Printed in Canada

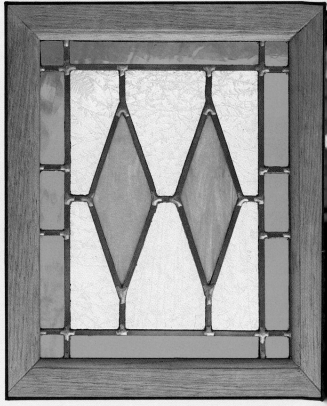

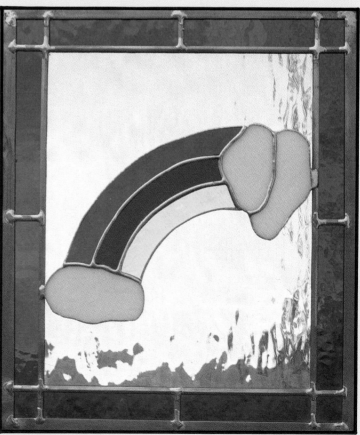

e-mail: info@wardellpublications.com – website: www.wardellpublications.com

INTRODUCTION TO STAINED GLASS

A TEACHING MANUAL

Written by
Randy Wardell &
Judy Huffman

Editors
Bill Dick
Eric Haughton
Robert Huffman

Photography
Randy Wardell
Judy Huffman

Pattern Editor and Production
Linda Holmes

Typesetting and Layout
Steve Campbell, Janet Moore
Randy Wardell

Special Thanks

Bruce Bath
John Grindrod
Mary Hurtzig

Eric Jaegge
Bob Kirk
Hillary Kent-Andrews

Lou Reda
Ron Ternoway
Carole Wardell

Printed in Canada
by Thorn Press

Published by

Wardell
PUBLICATIONS INC

To receive our electronic newsletter or to send suggestions please contact us
by EMail at: info@wardellpublications.com or visit our web site at: www.wardellpublications.com

PREFACE

The stained glass industry has grown by leaps and bounds over the past 20 years. Stained glass lamps and windows are found almost everywhere in restaurants, offices and homes. Some can be attributed to professional studios but many more are constructed by part time hobby crafters in a home workshop. All that is required is a few tools, some glass supplies, a little instruction and you too will be producing exciting stained glass art.

Introduction to Stained Glass with its step by step instruction is designed to be a self-teaching manual. It describes in detail the tools, supplies and techniques necessary to create exciting projects. Included are full-size patterns for sun catchers, windows, lampshades and three dimensional projects, all specifically designed for the beginning crafter. These projects can be constructed quickly and easily and make attractive and inexpensive gifts.

This textbook will be of particular interest to anyone taking a stained glass course. It will also prove essential as a workshop reference manual for review of specific problems once the course is completed.

It is hoped that with the assistance provided by this book, the stained glass artisan of today will create the heirlooms of tomorrow.

Happy glass crafting.

Cataloguing in Publication Data
Wardell, Randy A (Randy Allan), 1954-
Introduction to Stained Glass: A Teaching Manual
Includes Index
ISBN 0-919985-04-1
1. Glass craft. 2. Glass painting and staining.
3. Glass craft– Patterns.
I. Title
TT298.W37 1985 748.5'028'2 C85-098882-9

CONTENTS

The origin of glass is unclear. Shards of glass dated to 7000 B.C. have been unearthed in Egypt and Iraq. Sometime between 3000 and 1500 B.C., Egyptian craftsmen developed a reliable system for glass making. The earliest stained glass window to have survived intact is an 11th century A.D. face of Christ. Originally installed in the Wissembourg Abbey, it is now on display in a museum in Strasbourg, West Germany.

From the 11th to the 16th century, stained glass went through many changes. Generally speaking, it was reserved for religious use, as it was believed the light which beamed through these windows was spiritual light from heaven.

The 17th and 18th centuries are referred to as the period of destruction. During these centuries, many beautiful works of stained glass art were destroyed by religious puritans and fundamentalists who objected to the way biblical images were depicted. This unfavorable atmosphere reduced the demand for colored glass to such an extent, that by the mid 17th century it was virtually unobtainable.

A renewed interest in stained glass began in Europe in the early 19th century. The art of manufacturing colored glass had to be revived and in the mid 1800's glassmakers started reproducing "antique glass." Meanwhile many glass workshops in the United States were experimenting in the production of new types of colored glass. Two of these American glassmakers, John La Farge and Louis Comfort Tiffany, developed and produced a glass called *opalescent*. This glass differed from the traditional clear European glass, in that it featured a translucent, 'milky' quality.

The art nouveau movement provided a breath of new life for the stained glass trade. The movement spread throughout Europe and North America in the early part of the 20th century. The lamps and windows produced by the L.C. Tiffany Company and other firms increased the popularity of stained glass, bringing its beauty into homes, offices and public buildings.

Stained glass went through a period of obscurity from the 1930's to the 1950's, but it was never a 'lost art.' It is safe to say that the art of Stained Glass is more popular today than at any time in its history.

English stained glass window from the 14th century A.D. (courtesy: The Corning Museum of Glass)

Group of cast and core formed glass objects, L to R: Flask, Lentoid Flask, Goblet, Ewer, Vase. Egyptian from 1460-1085 B.C. (Courtesy: The Corning Museum of Glass)

An excellent example of a Landscape Memorial Window executed by the Louis C. Tiffany Co. circa 1900. (Courtesy: The Corning Museum of Glass)

Introduction to Stained Glass

Antique Glass making— a sketch by T.R. Davis published in Harper's Weekly, Jan. 1884. (Courtesy: The Corning Museum of Glass)

GLASS MAKING

Modern glass making is an extremely refined process. Glass is made basically from silica sand, limestone and soda ash. The mixture is put into a glass furnace and heated to approximately 3000º F, until the raw materials melt into a liquid which can be formed into glass sheets. To color the glass, various metal oxides are added to the raw materials during the glass making operation. These include selenium or gold for red, yellow and pink; cobalt for blue and sulphur for amber. The final price of the glass is influenced by the cost of these oxides. The expense is most evident when purchasing hot colors (red, yellow, orange, pink), as gold and selenium are expensive ingredients.

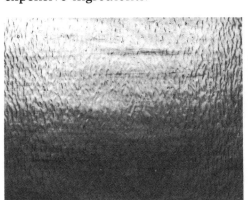

Granite-Back

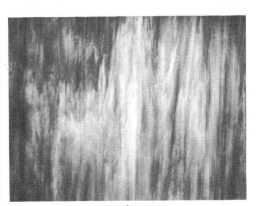

Opalescent   *Opalescent*

Streaky Cathedral

STAINED GLASS

The three main categories of 'Stained Glass' are Cathedral, Opalescent and Antique. To make Cathedral and Opalescent glass, a small batch of molten glass is poured onto a heated steel table and rolled into a sheet. The third type, Antique glass, is so named because it is formed using an old process. The glassmaker first blows a large cylinder of glass and lets it cool. Next the ends are removed and the cylinder is cut down one side. It is then placed in a flattening oven to unroll. Once the glass has flattened, or in the case of Cathedral and Opalescent, has been rolled into a sheet, it is sent through an annealing oven or *lehr* for gradual cooling.

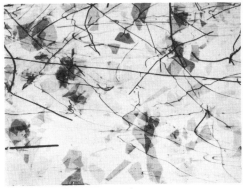

Fractures and streamers

Ripple-Back   *Glue Chipped*   *Wispy Opalescent*

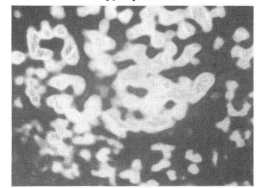

Ring-Mottled

Seedy Cathedral

CATHEDRAL— This transparent glass is available in one color or combinations of colors[1] and with various textures such as seedy, (i.e. containing bubbles), hammered, rippled, granite back and numerous others. The automated production of this glass enables it to be manufactured with a high quality at low cost making it a popular choice of professionals and enthusiasts alike.

OPALESCENT— This glass generally contains streaks and swirls which give it movement and life when lit from behind. This machine made glass has a 'milky' appearance, and is most commonly used for lamps, since it diffuses the light from the bulb.
    'Wispy Opals'— An opalescent glass made by limiting the amount of chemical that produces the 'milky' quality. This results in transparent streaks throughout the sheet.

ANTIQUE— Although some 'antique glass' is manufactured in the United States, most is imported from Europe. It is distinctive due to its brilliance and color intensity; this, along with the vast range of colors, has made it a favorite for many artists. The labour intensive hand-blowing process makes this glass more expensive than machine-made glass.
    'Drawn-Antique' ('Semi' or 'New' Antique)— A machine made, highly transparent glass which is similar in appearance to antique but lacks the brilliance and depth. This glass is an excellent choice for many projects since it is available in a wide range of colors and is less expensive than antique glass.
    You will find many variations within all the categories. They include ring-mottled, streaky, fracture, flashed, crackle, irridised, glue-chip and granite-back, to mention only a few. With time you will learn to identify and use the many varieties.

---

[1] Glass made by combining two or more colors of transparent glass is called 'Streaky Cathedral.'

GLASS NUGGETS— Nuggets are glass globs which have a smooth rounded top and a flat bottom. Unlike jewels, nuggets are free-formed, producing inconsistent shapes and sizes. They can be wrapped with foil or lead to represent grapes, cherries, balloons, eyes, noses and countless other adornments.

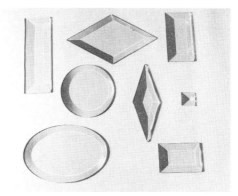

GLASS JEWELS— Jewels are made by pressing molten colored glass into a mold. They come in a variety of shapes, sizes and colors and can be smooth or multi-faceted. Jewels were used extensively in Victorian windows to add qualities of depth and character. Today, artists incorporate them into many designs including lamps, jewelry boxes, sun catchers and windows.

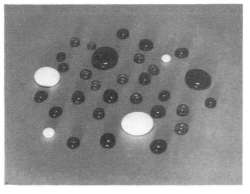

GLASS BEVELS— These are pieces of glass which have been ground by special machines, creating a slanted border on all sides. These beveled edges refract the sunlight into dazzling rainbows, making bevels a popular choice for panels in doors and windows. They can be expensive because of the time-consuming beveling process. There are many pre-packaged bevel clusters as well as standard shapes available.

COLOR SELECTION

The exciting and mesmerising colors of stained glass are without a doubt the reason for its existence. It was the color that lured most of us to this art form in the first place. A well-planned color arrangement can make or break a project. Knowing this, you must approach the selection of colors with the utmost respect.

There are few hard and fast rules governing color schemes. Much of it is personal preference. As the old line goes, "I don't know art but I know what I like." A good point to remember is that it is you who must build the project and ultimately take responsibility for it. Take time, listen to advice, and make a selection based on your own feelings.

The following is a set of general guidelines which may help you with this critical task:

1. PLAN out your color scheme before you visit the glass supply studio. Make a small sketch of your project and color it using pencil crayons or water paints. It may be helpful to make several copies and try different color combinations.

2. BALANCE the colors across the entire design. Too often, colors are inserted because they "go with the drapes" or "it's my favourite color," rather than to enhance the color scheme. Stand back from your color sketch to see if the combination is effective.

3. THEME— It is often useful to choose a dominant color and stick to the hues which complement your choice. Often the design itself or the function of your project will dictate the color theme. Try to keep your color selections simple, as too many colors can be disastrous.

4. TEXTURE- It is difficult to visualize textures in a color sketch, but texture can be an important part of a stained glass design. It is often very effective simply to change a texture to distinguish one particular area from another rather than to change a color. Many windows have no color; instead, they are constructed of various textured glasses which have been arranged to strengthen the design.

Once you have a fairly solid idea of your color scheme you are ready to visit your local glass shop. You will find a seemingly endless variety of colors, textures and types of glass. This can be intimidating. Start by picking the dominant colors and build around them, staying as true as possible to your color plan. **Note:** The glass should be viewed in light conditions similar to the real conditions that will exist when the project is installed, e.g. mirrors on a wall, artificially lit panel, incandescent bulb in a lamp. Sometimes it is necessary to arrange the glass pieces on your drawing roughly as they will appear, then stand back and look for the rhythm and balance. It will take time to select the colors for your project, but that's the way the creative process works.

CHAPTER TWO   TOOLS OF THE TRADE

As in any craft, the adage of using the proper tool for a proper job applies. In this chapter we will list and explain the various tools you will require to complete your projects. Many of the tools are available in several models and they vary in price and quality. Ask your supplier to explain the specific models they carry.

GLASS CUTTERS

There is an extensive variety of glass cutters available today. In recent years many inventors have introduced advanced design cutters for the glass trade. We will discuss only general categories of cutters. You should ask your instructor or supplier for their recommendations.

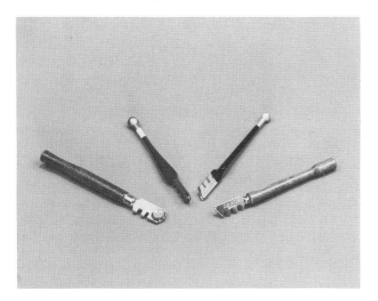

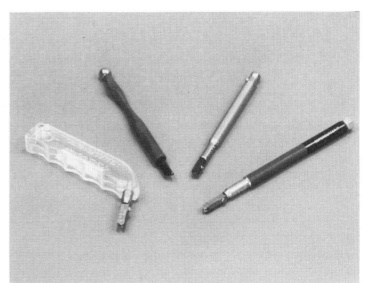

STANDARD STEEL WHEEL CUTTERS— These are the most common cutters available. They are manufactured with metal, wood or plastic handles in a variety of shapes. The main advantage of this cutter is the low cost. The disadvantage is that the wheel will not stay sharp long and must be lubricated before each score.

STANDARD CARBIDE WHEEL CUTTERS— These cutters are similar to those described above but have carbide wheels. Because of the carbide, the wheels stay sharp for a much longer period of time. However, these cutters are more expensive than the standard steel wheel cutter, and these also must be lubricated before each score.

SELF LUBRICATING CARBIDE WHEEL CUTTER— This glass cutter is superior to the others listed. Although it is a more expensive tool, it will pay for itself through less accidental glass breakage. The handle of the cutter holds the lubricant and supplies it to the cutter wheel automatically. The small diameter carbide wheel requires far less pressure when scoring and will outlast other cutters by a wide margin.

PLIERS

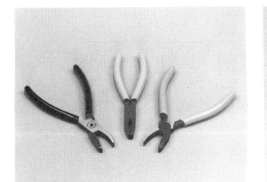
Combination Pliers

Grozing Pliers

Breaking Pliers

Running Pliers

COMBINATION BREAKER-GROZER PLIERS— These versatile pliers are the most useful for glass crafting. They are almost as important to a good glass break as the cutter. One jaw is straight and one is curved, and both have serrated teeth for grozing. If your budget limits you to one pair of pliers these are the ones you should purchase.

BREAKING PLIERS— Both jaws on these pliers are straight and somewhat wider. When the jaws are closed they meet only at the tip. This allows the jaw tip to grip the glass at the score.

GROZING PLIERS— These pliers have narrow jaws both with serrated teeth for shaping the glass. Unlike the breaking pliers, the jaws meet parallel when closed. This limits their use to grozing only. (See Page 25 for Grozing.)

RUNNING PLIERS— These are pliers with special jaws designed to make a score run (break) across the glass. The centering mark provided on the top jaw is aligned to the score and when the handles are squeezed pressure is exerted from under the score, breaking the glass. They are used for breaking out long, thin strips of glass, and are often helpful when breaking out curves.

SOLDERING IRONS & ACCESSORIES

A proper soldering iron is a very important piece of equipment. There are many makes and models available, but you must consider the following when purchasing yours.

1. It should be between 60 and 150 watts (preferably 80 to 100 watts).
2. It should be lightweight since it must be held for extended periods of time.
3. It should have a steel-clad chisel point tip between 1/8" and 3/8", preferably interchangable.

Ask your instructor or supplier for their recommendations, since it is impossible for us to list all suitable brands of soldering irons.

Most soldering irons become too hot for stained glass soldering if simply plugged into a standard electrical outlet. An overheated iron will make soldering difficult, will melt the lead came, and will cause the glass to crack. Here are two solutions to this overheating problem.

1. Temperature Controlled Iron— This soldering iron has an internal mechanism designed to limit the temperature to a range between 600° F and 800° F.

2. Rheostat Temperature Controller— This device controls the amount of voltage received by a soldering iron. When the voltage is lower, it has the effect of lowering the maximum temperature the iron can reach.

Soldering iron stand— For the sake of safety, when you put your iron down, always place it in (or on) a stand, especially when it is hot.

Iron Cleaning Sponge— This is a heat resistant sponge that can be purchased by itself or with a holder for your iron. To clean a steel-tipped iron, dampen the sponge and wipe your iron across it periodically during soldering. NOTE: If your iron has a copper tip (not steel-clad) you should ask your instructor or supplier how to clean and tin it.

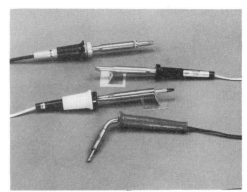

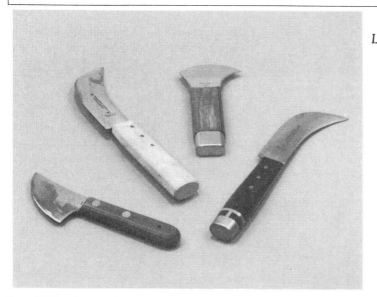

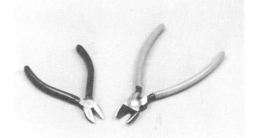

Lead Knives

Lead Dykes

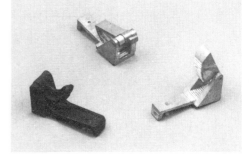

Lead Vises

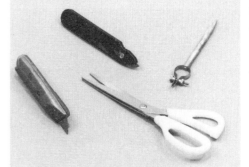

Utility Knife,
Pattern Knives
and Shears

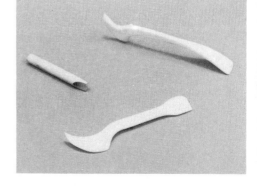

Lathekins

Hammers, Nails
and Wire Brush

Lead Knife— This is the professional's choice for cutting lead came. You will find several different styles but, as with any good knife, you must pay for quality. The less costly knives may look the same but will not hold a sharp edge for long.

Lead Dyke— This cutter resembles an electrician's diagonal wire cutter. It is, however, distinctly different in that only one side of the blades are beveled (sharpened). This allows the lead to be cut with one end completely flat while leaving the other end pointed. There are several drawbacks to this tool: 1. You must cut the pointed end off each time. 2. It doesn't cut lead at an angle and 3. It doesn't cut wide lead cleanly.

Lead Vise— This tool is used to secure one end of the lead came, allowing you to stretch it from the other end with pliers. It can be fastened with a screw to one end of your work bench.

Lead Pattern Shears— These shears are best described as three bladed scissors. They are used to cut patterns for lead, removing a 5/64" strip of paper to allow space for the heart of the lead.

Utility Knife— This item is also called a carpet knife or matte knife. It can be adapted for cutting patterns by placing a cardboard spacer between two blades and securing it with two-sided tape or glue. This knife can be purchased at a hardware store.

Lathekin (Fid)— An inexpensive but essential tool for lead working. It is used to open the channel of lead and to push the glass pieces into place. In the copper foil technique it is used to *burnish* (flatten) the foil to the glass edges. Lathekins are available in wood or plastic.

Horseshoe Nails— These nails are flat on two sides and are used to hold the glass pieces in place while you are assembling your project. Do not use common round nails as they will gouge the soft lead came.

Hammer— A small lightweight hammer is best. It is used for tacking the horseshoe nails to the work surface and helps to seat and tighten the glass in the lead came channel.

Small Wire Brush— This is a toothbrush size tool used to clean tarnished lead joints prior to soldering.

16

Introduction to Stained Glass

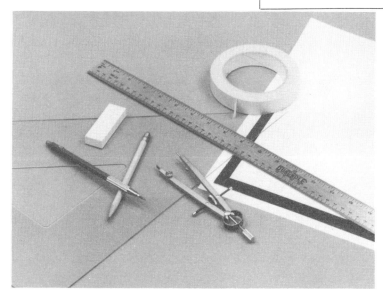

DRAWING EQUIPMENT

Listed here are some basic drawing tools. With these you can produce an accurate drawing which is essential to a well-made project.

- drawing square
- carbon paper
- ruler (18" to 36")
- pattern card paper
- pencil and eraser
- drawing paper
- drawing compass
- masking tape

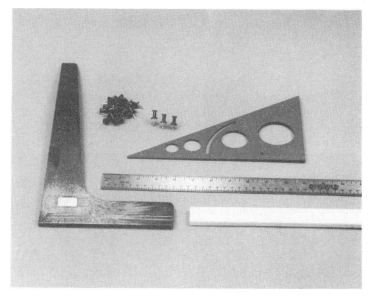

Straight Edge— When making a straight score, use a straight edge as a guide for your cutter. A metal or wooden ruler between 12"-24" is ideal. To prevent the straight edge from slipping when scoring the glass, apply an adhesive cork strip to the back. A thin layer of silicone sealant or plastic electrical tape will also reduce slippage.

Push Pins— To secure foiled glass pieces for soldering, use plastic-ended push pins. Normally used as bulletin board tacks, they can be purchased at a stationery store.

SAFETY EQUIPMENT

Stained glass crafting is a relatively safe hobby if precautions are taken. The following items should be used when necessary:

Safety glasses— Glasses should be worn when scoring and breaking glass. They are necessary when grozing or grinding as these operations cause small glass chips to fly up from the glass.

Bench brush— Clean the work surface and keep it free of small glass chips with a suitable brush or wisk broom.

Bandaids— ALWAYS patch up small cuts with a bandaid to keep out flux, dirt and lead.

Ventilation— When soldering you should provide good air circulation by setting up a fan to draw the fumes away. If this is not possible, obtain a breathing mask to keep from inhaling the fumes when you are working.

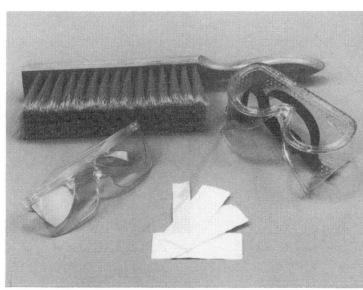

GRINDING & SHAPING EQUIPMENT

No matter how accomplished your cutting skills become you will find the need to remove small bits of glass to make your project fit better. Here is some equipment to make this task easier:

Carborundum Stone - A coarse sharpening stone (the kind used to sharpen axes or knives) can be used to remove rough edges of glass. It is best to keep the stone wet with water to help prevent chipping the glass edges.

Glass Grinders - These machines are the ultimate tool for final glass shaping and clean-up. The grinding bit can remove everything from slightly jagged edges to 1/4" or more of glass, quickly and easily. The water-fed diamond-embedded grinding bit virtually eliminates glass edge chipping. The bits are available from 1/4" diameter, which enables you to get to the difficult inside cut areas, to 3/4" & 1" diameter bits for faster grinding. The

1/4" bit even has diamond grit on the top surface to allow you to grind a hole through glass. You will find a variety of other bits available for specialized applications. Several grinder models are available from hobby to professional duty models. Ask your glass supply store for a hands on demonstration of one of these remarkable machines.

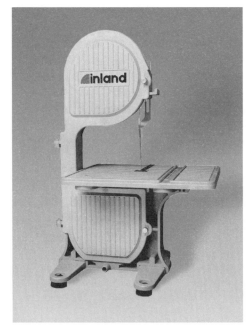

Glass Saws - This category of cutting tools include, band saws, ring saws and mini-table saws. They give you the freedom to cut any shape that you can imagine and they do away with the need to grind after cutting. In addition they reduce frustration and save glass by eliminating errant glass breaks. These saws are particularly useful on drapery glass and other heavy textures, which are difficult to cut with a standard cutter. However, they will not replace your traditional glass cutter and grinder, and should be considered an accessory tool for creative glass work.

Solder— Solder is an *alloy* (mixture of metals) used to fasten one metal to another. When heated, it melts and bonds to the surface. The most common alloys used for stained glass are 60/40 (60% tin and 40% lead) and 50/50 (50% tin and 50% lead). Both will work on lead or foil. However, 50/50 is less expensive and generally is used for soldering lead. The properties of the 60/40 alloy make it easier to use with copper foil. **CAUTION:** Rosin or acid core solder is not recommended as the flux it contains does not work well for lead or foil.

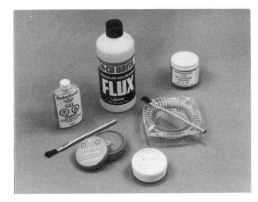

Flux— This must be applied to the lead or copper foil just prior to soldering to remove oxides from the surface. Without fluxing, solder would not stick to the metal. There are many different brands of flux available in liquid, gel and paste form. Most are made from zinc chloride and acid. Caution must be taken when using them since they are corrosive. Liquid or gel fluxes are preferred as they smoke and burn less and clean off more easily. To avoid spilling the container of flux, pour a small amount into a glass dish or ash tray to use when soldering. Paste flux is often used for lead soldering and repairs. Apply flux sparingly with a small brush (flux brush).

WORK SURFACE

Marking Pen— A fine, felt tip permanent ink marker (not water-soluble) is used to trace around your pattern onto the glass. If a water-soluble ink pen is used, the mark could be accidentally erased. For dark glass use a white ink marker or white china pencil which can be purchased from your supplier. Use fingernail polish remover or rubbing alcohol to remove permanent ink from the surface of the glass.

Lubricant— This keeps the cutter wheel rolling smoothly and helps rid the wheel housing of small glass particles. Kerosene is the lubricant usually recommended by cutter manufacturers although a mixture of kerosene and light oil is often used. Specially-formulated water-soluble cutter lubricants are available from many suppliers.

Wire— When forming hanging loops or reinforcing the edge of a lamp or a window, use uninsulated brass or copper wire from 14 to 20 gauge.

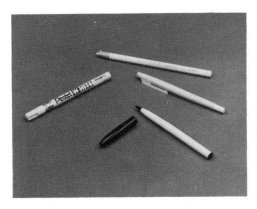

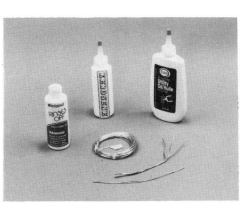

Work Board- Plywood or particle board (1/2" or 3/4") makes a good work surface. The size of board will depend on the space you have available. A good starter size is 2'x4'. It is important to have your work table at a suitable height (just below the waist) so you will be comfortable for long work periods. The work board must lie on a sturdy, flat surface. Keep your bench brush handy at all times to keep the working area clean.

When constructing small copper foil projects, you may find it convenient to have a small (12"x 12") workboard to allow movement for soldering. Choose a soft material such as pressed paper board or plywood so the push pins will stick in easily.

Lead Came— Strips of lead extruded with a channel on one or two sides are referred to as, *U* or *H* lead came. The glass is fitted into the channels and the lead becomes the backbone of the stained glass window. Came is purchased in six foot lengths and the crown widths range from 1/8" to 3/4". The most common widths are 3/16", 7/32", 1/4", and 3/8". The crowns can be either flat or round.

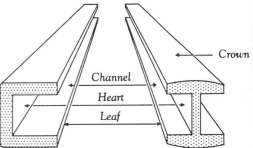

Cementing— This is the final stage in construction of a leaded panel. Cement is forced between the lead channel and the glass to strengthen and weatherproof a window. Pre-mixed cement, available at most suppliers, is comprised of metal sash putty, paint thinner, Plaster of Paris and a black colorant.

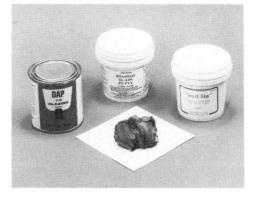

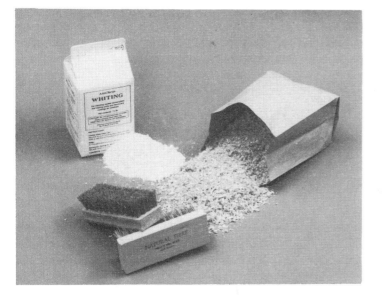

Whiting— Powdered calcium carbonate (chalk) is brushed on to the panel after cementing to help dry the cement, darken the leads and clean the panel. Plaster of Paris or sawdust can be used as substitutes.

Brushes— You will require two natural-bristled scrubbing brushes. Use one brush to force cement between the glass and lead, the other to clean the panel once the whiting is applied. These brushes can be purchased at most suppliers.

COPPER FOIL SUPPLIES

Copper Foil— This is a very thin copper sheet (similar in thickness to aluminum foil) with an adhesive back. Thirty-six yard rolls of copper foil tape can be purchased in widths between 1/8" and 1/2". It is wrapped around the outside edges of glass pieces and acts as a soldering base.

Foil Dispenser— Copper foil often becomes entangled when being unrolled. A dispenser will solve this problem and allow easy access to the foil.

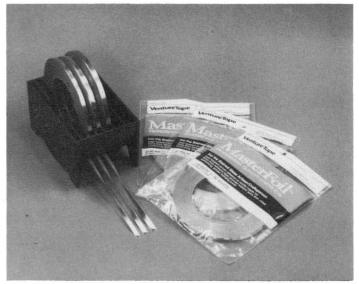

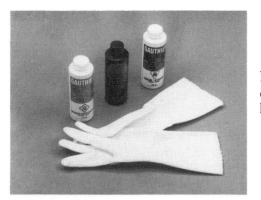

Patina— This chemical will change the color of solder to copper or black depending on the type of patina used. Special patinas can be obtained for use on lead came.

Foiling Machine— There are many models of foil wrapping machines, both manually-operated and motor driven. These will assist in the tedious task of foil wrapping. They are especially useful when you have a project with a large number of pieces. They require practice to run efficiently but once mastered save a considerable amount of time.

BASIC SHOPPING LIST

Brushes
Carborundum stone
Cement
Copper foil
Flux
Flux Brush
Glass cutter
Glass— Clear- (2 or 3mm)
   - 2 square feet for practice cutting
   - Stained Glass—
    See project material list
Horseshoe Nails (2 Dozen)
Lathekin
Lead— U and H style—
    See project material list
Lead Knife or Dyke
Lead Vise
Marking Pen
Patina
Pliers
Push Pins (2 Dozen)
Solder (minimum 1/2 lb.)
Soldering Iron
Whiting or sawdust
Wire

ITEMS FOUND AROUND THE HOUSE

Bandaids
Bench brush
Black Electrician tape
Cutter lubricant
Drawing equipment
Glass (ash) tray for flux
Glazing lath (1/2" x 1" wood trim)
Hammer
Masking tape
Needle nose pliers
Safety type glasses
Scissors
Small nails
Stainless steel or brass pot scrubber
Steel Wool (fine 000)
Straight edge or yard stick
Tin snips or sheet metal shears
Utility or Matte knife and blades
White bond glue
Wire cutters
Workboard
Xacto Knife

THEORY— WHY GLASS BREAKS

The term glass cutting is in fact a misnomer. When you score the glass, what you are really doing is creating a minute crack or fissure, called a *score*, directly under the cutting wheel. When pressure is exerted on this fissure a 'chain reaction' starts and the glass breaks along the score line.

To execute an ideal score, a consistent pressure on the cutting wheel is essential. Too much pressure will cause the fissure to radiate into the glass at many different angles. You can't see this, but when the break is attempted the crack will start in one fissure then attempt to *jump* to another, often missing altogether only to shoot off across the glass anywhere it pleases. Conversely, too little pressure while scoring does not create a deep enough fissure and the break will be unsuccessful or sporadic at best.

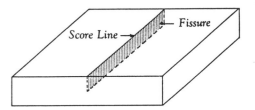

The fissure can be seen in clear glass by looking at the score line held at an angle.

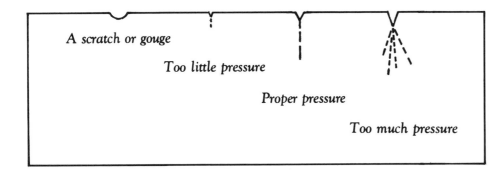

HOLDING THE GLASS CUTTER

There are many ways to hold a glass cutter. The photographs show a few of the most popular methods. Try out each one and settle on the style you feel is right for you. Whichever manner you choose, always keep the cutter wheel perpendicular to the glass. It is best to stand while cutting to make it easier to transfer pressure directly from your shoulder to the cutting wheel. With practice you will adopt a position which you find the most comfortable.

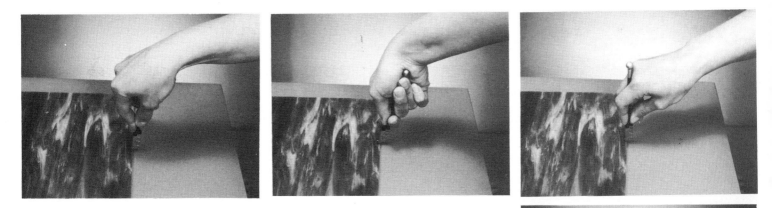

A scratch or gouge

Too little pressure

Proper pressure

Too much pressure

A comparison of scratches and various scores as they would be seen in a cross-section of glass

Introduction to Stained Glass

Before each score, lubricate the cutter wheel, make sure the glass is free from dirt and your cutting board clear of glass chips. When cutting stained glass, check that you are scoring the correct side of the glass (usually the smoothest and shiniest). For greater stability and a better line of sight, you should be standing in a comfortable position with your work directly in front of you.

Note: Wear safety glasses to protect your eyes from glass chips.

For an exercise in practice cutting, obtain about two square feet of single or double strength (2 or 3mm) standard clear glass. Follow the steps outlined in this section, scoring and breaking this glass into small pieces. Continue scoring and breaking until you get 'the feel' for glass cutting.

Step 1: Hold your cutter in your 'tool' hand using the method most comfortable for you. Place your other hand on the glass to hold it from moving and use the thumb to provide a guide to your cutter.

Step 2: Place the cutter wheel on the glass about 1/8" in from edge closest to you. Place the thumb of your guide hand behind the cutter head to prevent it from rolling back off the glass edge.

Step 3: Apply firm pressure downward onto the cutter with your cutting hand and push it at a constant speed across the surface of the glass with your guide hand. If you are scoring correctly, you will feel the wheel *rolling* with *a slight resistance* across the glass and hear a *scritching* noise. Continue to score completely to the far edge but ease up on the pressure as you score off to avoid chipping. **(Caution:** Do not become too dependent on the noise, as a carbide or new cutting wheel will not make a sound on certain colored glass.)

Step 4: Observe your score. If there are small glass chips popping from the score line, or if it appears gritty, then you have exerted too much pressure on the cutter. The score should appear as a clean, even, faint white line. NEVER go over the same score twice as this will damage the cutter wheel and does not improve the score.

Note: Although it may sound obvious, you must always score from one edge of the glass completely across to the other edge to get the desired piece. *See Diagram:* For example, to get the desired piece (shaded area) you cannot simply score from A to C and then from C to D (a 90° break is impossible). You must first score completely across from A to B, break out the score and then score from C to D and break out this score.

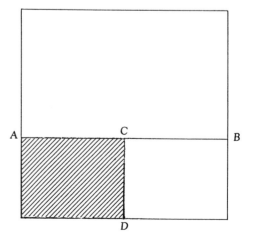

BREAKING OUT THE SCORE

Once you have a satisfactory score on your glass piece, it can be broken out in several ways depending on the shape of the cut (straight, inside or outside curve). In most cases, it will be helpful to keep your elbows tight to your sides and the glass in-close to your body to give your hands good leverage.

BREAKING WITH HANDS

1. Form your hands into fists and place the glass between your thumbs and index fingers with the score line between your thumbs. Your fingers should be clenched underneath the glass with knuckles touching.

2. Hold the glass firmly at the end of the score, apply a quick even pressure by pulling outward then roll the top part of your hands by spreading your thumbs apart. This movement applies pressure *down* on each side of the score with the thumbs and *up* from underneath the score line with the knuckles. Your hands should snap away from each other on completion of the break.

BREAKING USING PLIERS

1. Form one hand into a fist and place the glass between your thumb and index finger and close to the score line. With your tool hand position the plier jaws so that they are 90 degrees to the score (not touching), and as close to the end of the score as possible. When using combination breaker/grozer pliers the flat jaw should be on the top side of the glass.

2. Hold the glass firmly with your hand and apply an even pressure by pulling outward and snap down with the pliers. If the glass breaks unevenly and leaves a jagged edge, it will require some grozing (see Page 25— Grozing).

3. Sometimes the glass piece may be too small to hold in your hand and apply enough pressure to break apart. Position a second pair of pliers directly opposite the first, 90 degrees to the score and as close to the end of the score as possible. Apply a quick even pressure by pulling outward then down with the pliers.

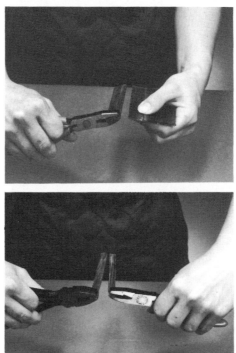

BREAKING BY TAPPING UNDER THE SCORE

Generally speaking, tapping is used to crack the score when breaking out a difficult cut. (E.g. deep inside curves) Tapping should be used with discretion as it can damage the glass and may cause the break to be jagged. The proper procedure is to hold the glass securely on both sides of the score in one hand and, starting at the end, tap directly under the score with the ball end of your cutter. Once a small crack starts, tap along the score until it has run to the end. Finish the break by hand or with pliers.

BREAKING USING RUNNING PLIERS

1. For large pieces lay the glass flat on your bench and let the end of the score overhang slightly. Align the guide mark on the top jaw of the running pliers with the score and in ½" from the edge.

2. Gently squeeze the pliers and the break will run (follow) along the score line. If the break travels only part way along the score, as may happen with long narrow pieces or severe curves, move the pliers to the opposite end and repeat.

SCORING USING A STRAIGHT EDGE

Making a straight score using a metal or wooden guide is often the most difficult cutting technique to master. The main reason for this seems to be that concentration is directed at following the straight edge rather than at making a proper score.

1. Position the straight edge along the pattern line, making the proper allowance for the cutter head. Make a 'dry run' (apply no pressure) along the straight edge with your cutter to check your stance and the position of the edge.

2. Press down on the straight edge to hold it from slipping. Make an even consistent score using either a push or pull action (both will work, however it is usually easier and more accurate to pull). The most common mistake is to turn the cutter into the guide while scoring. You must always keep the cutter head parallel to the straight edge.

GROZING

Often a score does not break out smoothly, and you need to remove small bits of glass. This is done with your grozer or breaker-grozer pliers.

1. Use the tip of the jaw (sometimes just the corner) to grasp a small protrusion and snap it off.

2. To remove irregular edges insert the glass edge into the jaws of the pliers (at 90 degrees) and drag the serrated teeth across it several times.

3. Use the edge of the jaw to grasp the unwanted protrusion and twist the pliers away to chew it off. **Note:** You could use a glass grinder instead of grozing and, although it may take a little longer, will usually produce a more satisfactory result.

CUTTING INSIDE CURVES

Cutting a deep inside curve into glass is tricky even for an experienced crafter. An inside curve can be so severe that it is virtually impossible to break out. When practicing this skill, give yourself realistic challenges at first and build up to deeper and deeper curves. It will take time and patience to master this skill, so don't give up easily.

Note: When cutting to a pattern that contains a deep inside curve, position the curve as close as possible to the edge of the glass sheet. Score and break out the curve before cutting the piece away from your main sheet of glass. This will allow the pattern to be repositioned if the curve fails to break out correctly.

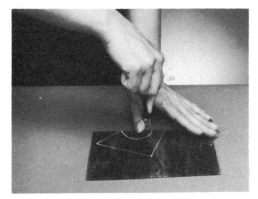

Step 1: Make an initial score following the inside curve of the pattern. Do not attempt to break this score out yet.

Step 2: Make a shallow concave second (relief) score, starting at one corner of the curved edge and score across to the opposite corner.

Step 3: Start the next relief score slightly farther inside the curve and score across to the opposite corner. Continue making shallow concave relief scores until all inside glass is scored as shown.

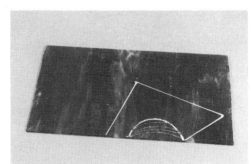

Step 4: Hold the glass securely with one hand. Position the grozing pliers at the corner of the most shallow relief score and break it out in the same direction as scored.

Step 5: Continue breaking out the relief scores in sequence until the inside curve is complete. If a corner broke off or the attempt failed entirely, you may not have made enough relief scores.

Note: If a curve is severe, it may be helpful to tap the glass under the score with the ball end of your cutter to start the crack.

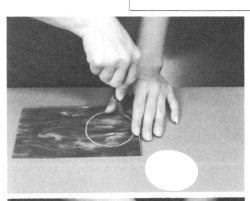

Step 1: Score completely around the circle or curve following the pattern line.

Step 2: Score a relief line on a tangent to the circle. Start at the glass edge and score up to meet the circle. Move the cutter part way around the circle and score from the circle to the opposite edge.

Step 3: Continue to move around the circle making relief scores from the circle to an edge. The size of circle will determine the number of relief scores necessary, but six to eight will usually be sufficient.

Step 4: Hold the glass firmly with your hand. Grasp the first segment with pliers and break it off by pulling outward and down.

Step 5: Continue breaking away the segments in sequence until the circle is complete. The glass will require grozing where the segments break unevenly and leave a jagged edge (see Page 25— Grozing).

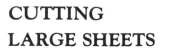

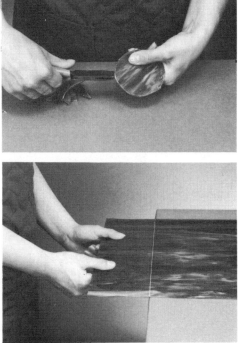

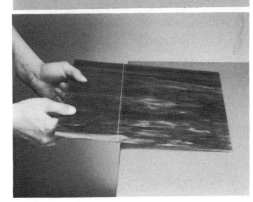

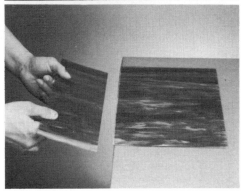

CUTTING LARGE SHEETS

Use this method to cut a sheet in half or to remove a 2" or larger strip.

Step 1: Score a straight line from one edge to the other using a straight edge. Refer to *Scoring Using A Straight Edge*, Page 25.

Step 2: Grasp the glass piece securely and carefully line the score up with the edge of the bench.

Step 3: Raise the end you are holding approximately one inch. (The other end of the glass must remain on the bench.)

Step 4: Quickly follow through downward with a snap. With any luck, you should be holding the separated glass piece in your hands.

PATTERN MAKING

The first task in constructing any project is to obtain a design completed to full size. With the many books and patterns available in full size (several patterns are in this book) finding a suitable project should be easy. As your skills develop and your interests expand, you will, no doubt, create your own patterns. For our purposes, however, we will concentrate on working with some of the full size patterns contained in this book.

The second task is to make the pattern. You will require the following materials and supplies: Pencil, ruler, 2 sheets of carbon paper, 1 sheet of drawing paper and 1 sheet of pattern card (e.g. Kraft paper, bristol board). **Note:** If you intend to cut your glass using the English method, pattern making and cutting will not be necessary. See Page 30 for the 'English Method'.

Step 1: Place the sheet of pattern card on your work table and then lay a sheet of carbon paper on top. Next, position the sheet of drawing paper and then another sheet of carbon paper. Finally, place your full size drawing on them all. Tape all corners securely to the work table (or pin them with push pins). Trace the drawing, using a sharp pencil and a straight ruler where possible. Press firmly (you're making three copies) and stay on the lines.

Step 2: Once you have finished tracing, each piece *must* be numbered. The best way to keep track of your pattern pieces is to code them according to your color selections. For example: amber A1-A8, red R9-R15, green G16-G20 and so on. Record this information on the outside edge of drawing. Mark any other important features directly on the pattern. For example: Mark the direction you want the glass streaks to flow with an arrow. Lift the bottom corners to ensure that you have traced and numbered all pieces.

Step 3: Dismantle the pattern assembly and set aside all copies except the bottom copy traced on pattern card. You must now consider the method of construction. This will determine how the pattern pieces are to be cut. If this project is for **LEAD ASSEMBLY,** a 5/64" strip of paper must be cut away between the pattern pieces. This will allow room between the glass pieces for the heart of the lead. The easiest way to accomplish this is to use special pattern shears or a two-bladed knife. (See Page 16). Cut your patterns down the middle of the lines and thereby removing them.

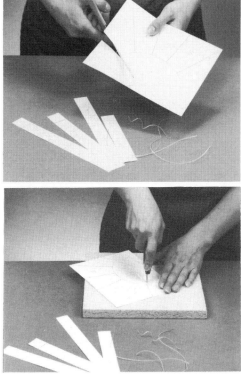

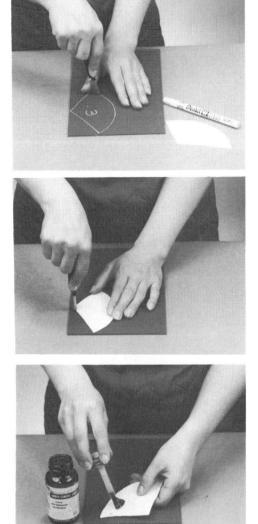

There are several ways to accurately cut your glass pieces following the patterns you create. The most popular methods are explained below.

Note: To protect a pattern or an assembly drawing that is to be used over and over, cover the surface with an adhesive backed clear vinyl sheet before cutting.

Step 4. If your project is for **FOIL ASSEMBLY,** remove a 1/32" strip of paper to allow for the copper foil and solder. To remove this strip, use foil pattern shears or a two-bladed knife with a 1/32" space. Many crafters will cut their foil patterns with standard scissors or an Xacto knife, and make the allowance while cutting the glass.

1. Trace with a felt-tipped pen: Use a felt-tipped glass pen and trace around the pattern directly onto the colored glass. Score the glass by following along the inside of the traced line. In other words, you must *cut the line away* so the marker line is on the waste glass when you break it off. By removing the line the glass piece will be exactly the same size as the pattern. If the glass is dark and you have difficulty seeing the tracing mark, use a white ink felt marker or a white china marker.

Note: This is the method we will be using in the step-by-step project assembly instructions that follow.

2. Hold the Pattern on the Glass: Hold the pattern piece on the glass surface with one hand and follow the edge of the pattern with the cutting wheel to score the glass. It takes practice to hold the pattern piece and make an exact score at the same time but once mastered this method can be very fast and accurate.

3. Glue Pattern to Glass: This is a variation on the holding method. (#2) Use rubber cement to coat the back side of your pattern piece and glue it directly to the glass surface. Once the glue has dried, follow the edge of the pattern with your cutting wheel to score the glass. This method is very accurate but since the patterns are coated with glue they are difficult to use for another project.

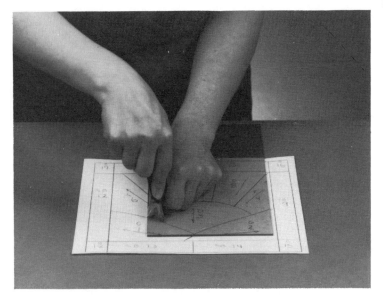

4. English Method: This method is used primarily for transparent glass. Place the colored glass directly on top of the full-sized drawing. Position the glass over the required pattern and score by following the pattern line while looking through the glass. Great care must be taken to cut on the inside of the line to make allowance for the heart of the lead. (See *Pattern Making*, Step 3.) When cutting dark glass, it would be necessary to place your drawing and glass on a light table (a glass-topped table illuminated from underneath).

5. Trace Directly onto the Glass: This is a variation on the English Method. Use carbon paper and trace through your working drawing directly onto the colored glass. You must remember to make an allowance for the heart of the lead while tracing and cutting.

Each of the foregoing methods has its advantages and disadvantages. You might choose to use different methods for different projects. In any event, discuss them with your instructor or supplier to find out what they recommend.

PHOTOCOPYING YOUR PATTERNS

In recent years the photocopier has come into very wide use for many applications. Local copy centers are opening everywhere offering services that include enlarging and reduction of your originals. This opens up a multitude of possibilities for the stained glass crafter to alter the size of patterns quickly and easily. Enlarging is especially useful for free-form projects such as sun catchers or small panels due to the limitation in size, depending on the photocopier used.

There is, however, one note of caution concerning the use of photocopiers (other than possible copyright infringements). Most photocopiers do not make exact copies of the original. While the copy is very close, the mechanics of the copying process introduces some amount of distortion that can be disastrous when constructing a three-dimensional project such as a lampshade. The distortion usually results in slightly enlarging (or reducing) the pattern in the vertical dimension to a greater degree than in the horizontal dimension. This does not mean you cannot use a photocopier for your lamp patterns but it does mean you must carefully measure each pattern component to verify that they will fit one to the other.

The traditional lead method is commonly referred to as *glazing* or *leading*. Simply described, it involves the assembly of glass pieces using lead *came* (channels) extruded in the shape of U or H. The lead came is cut and fitted between the glass pieces and finally soldered at the joints.

The lead came is not only the structural backbone of the window but is also a crucial element of the design. It is often the preferred method when constructing a window due to the strong linear quality the lead adds to the design. This quality can be emphasized by using several came widths within the same panel.

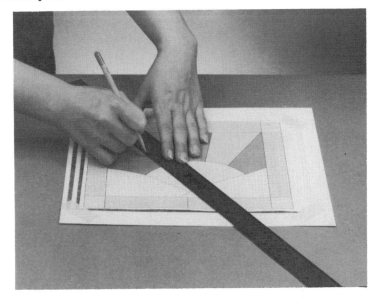

The question of possible lead poisoning is often asked by beginning crafters. Lead and lead oxides are not absorbed into the body through unbroken skin, but can enter through an open cut or by ingestion. The main forms of prevention are good hygiene and common sense. *ALWAYS* wash your hands thoroughly with soap and water after working with lead and *NEVER* eat while working at the glazing bench. *ALWAYS* protect an open cut with a bandaid and, of course, keep lead away from children.

Step 1: Trace your pattern as described in the section on *Pattern Making*. Be sure to cut the pattern pieces using the instruction for lead assembly as described on Page 28.

Step 2: Carefully trace the pattern onto the glass using a felt tip pen and cut the glass piece by scoring on the inside of the marker line. *You must always cut the line away* so the marker line is on the waste glass when you break it off. Check your glass piece with the pattern to verify that they are exactly the same size and shape. If the glass is not exact, you must grind it or cut it again. Adjust your cutting to be more precise when scoring the next piece.

Step 3: When all glass pieces are cut, place your working drawing on the work bench and tape it down. Cut two pieces of *glazing lath* (½" x 1" wood trim), one to fit along the left hand side and one for the bottom of your drawing. Nail them in place so the outside line of the drawing is just showing. If you are left handed, nail the lath on the right hand side.

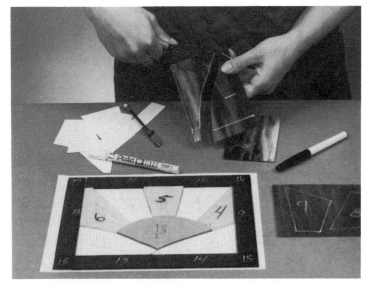

Step 4: You must decide which size (or sizes) of lead came to use for your project. Lead came is available in various widths but the most commonly used sizes are between 1/8" and 3/8" in both the U and H shape.

If your panel is to be installed in a frame, use a wide H lead (3/8" to 1/2") for the outside edges. This will allow the perimeter lead to show around the wood frame and can be trimmed somewhat if the panel grows a little during assembly. The use of wide H came will increase the overall size of your panel, and allowance must be made on the pattern to account for this.

If the panel is a free hanging piece, a U lead (3/16" to 3/8") should be used. The internal (H) lead size will depend on the overall size of the panel. Often the material list that accompanies a drawing will recommend the size of lead required. If you are unsure, ask your instructor or supplier for advice.

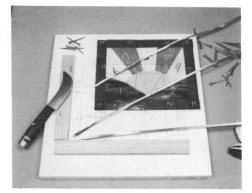

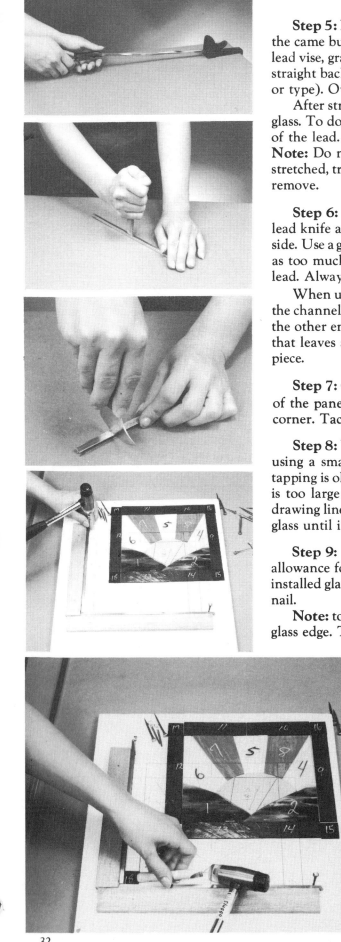

Step 5: Lead came must be stretched just prior to use. This not only straightens the came but also makes it more rigid. To stretch, place one end of the came in the lead vise, grasp the other end with pliers, turn as required to remove twists and pull straight back. A 6' length of lead will stretch between 3"-5" (depending on lead size or type). Overstretching will weaken the lead structure.

After stretching 'U' came, the channel must be opened sufficiently to accept the glass. To do this, insert your lathekin into the channel and pull it along the length of the lead.

Note: Do not stretch the lead until just before you are ready to use it and, once stretched, treat it with care as kinks and twists will be difficult (if not impossible) to remove.

Step 6: Cut the lead came for the outside edges of your project. When using a lead knife always cut 'H' lead on the *crown* (top) side and 'U' lead on the channel side. Use a gentle side-to-side motion while pressing straight down. Do not use force as too much pressure will crush the heart. Practice a few cuts on a scrap piece of lead. Always be sure to keep your lead knife sharp.

When using a lead dyke you must position the jaws 90⁰ to the lead and cut into the channel for both 'H' and 'U' came. Dykes leave one end of the lead cut flat and the other end pointed. Experiment on some scrap lead to find the side of the dyke that leaves a clean flat end. This is the side you will usually use to cut your lead piece.

Step 7: Cut two pieces of the edge lead, one for the bottom and one for the side of the panel. Place them on the drawing, along the lath and butt the ends at the corner. Tack them with horseshoe nails.

Step 8: Fit the corner glass piece into the channel and *gently tap* it into position using a small wood block (or wood lathekin) and a hammer. **Caution:** A little tapping is okay, however, if a piece is not seating properly it usually means the glass is too large and no amount of tapping will help. You should be able to see the drawing lines around the exposed edges of this glass piece. If not, grind or groze the glass until it fits properly.

Step 9: Measure and cut a piece of H lead to fit from edge to edge, making an allowance for the overlap of the adjoining lead channel. Place this lead against the installed glass piece and insert the next glass piece as shown. Tack with a horseshoe nail.

Note: to prevent chipping, place a small scrap of lead (preferably 'U') over the glass edge. Then tack the glass with the nail against the lead.

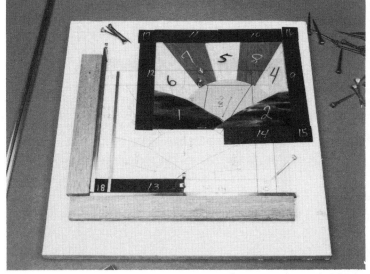

Introduction to Stained Glass

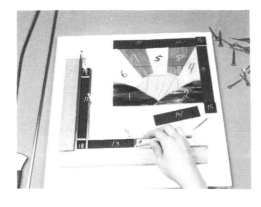

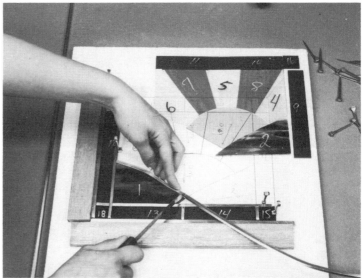

Step 10: Cut a short piece of 'H' lead to fit inside the border leads and against the corner glass piece. Use your lathekin to position the lead and seat the channel over the glass edge. Insert the next glass border piece according to your pattern and continue positioning lead and fitting glass until the side and bottom borders are complete. Be sure to secure all pieces with horseshoe nails.

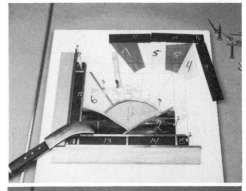

Step 11: Now begin assembly of the design section by inserting the bottom corner glass piece. Measure a lead by placing it along the glass edge and tightly against the border lead. Mark your lead with your knife about 1/16" shorter than the end of the glass. The lead is cut short to allow for the channel overlap of the adjoining lead. Depending on the angle of the adjoining lead, a miter (angled) cut may be necessary. Cut and place the lead into position.

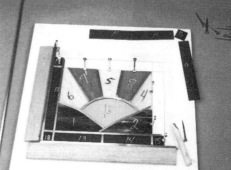

Step 12: As you continue along leading your project, some thought must be given to the logical sequence of placing the glass pieces. Always plan the order of the next two or three pieces you intend to fit. Continually make the following checks as you go: 1. Keep the project tight by *gently* tapping to seat the glass and leads using a wood block or lathekin and a hammer (with caution). 2. The drawing line must always be visible around the edge of each glass piece. 3. All lead joints must butt tightly against one another. 4. Be sure all glass pieces are secured with sufficient horseshoe nails to keep the work tight.

Step 13: When all the inside leading is complete, you must fit the outside edge lead onto the two remaining sides. Measure one lead for the top and cut it ½" longer than the panel. Butt it against the side lead and place it on the top edge; tack with nails. Cut the last lead to fit inside the top and bottom cames. Place it on the side and secure with nails.

Note: Two additional pieces of glazing lath could be cut and nailed against the outside to avoid damaging the leads with nails.

SOLDERING LEAD CAME

Soldering is required where two or more leads butt together. You will need your soldering iron, flux and solder to complete the project. (For details on these items see pages 15, 19, 20).

To prepare the panel for soldering, inspect all lead joints. If there are gaps in some, cut small scraps of leads to fill in spaces. If the leads are oxidized (corroded, not a shiny silver), clean them with a steel brush or by scraping with the edge of your lead knife. When all joints have passed the inspection, begin soldering.

Step 1: Apply flux to each joint with a flux brush. *Be careful* to brush the flux only on the area where solder is required as the hot molten solder will flow and stick to the lead wherever flux is applied.

Step 2: Place the end of the solder on the joint, touch the flat side of your soldering iron tip to it and melt the solder down onto the joint. Take away the solder roll and keep the iron down on the joint for a second longer, then pick the iron *straight up.* The solder should flow into a gently rounded bead. If it appears rough, place your iron tip back on the soldered joint and move it in a slow circular motion until the solder is completely molten. Pick the iron tip *straight up* again. **Note:** wherever you move the iron, the molten solder will follow, so don't move too far off the joint.

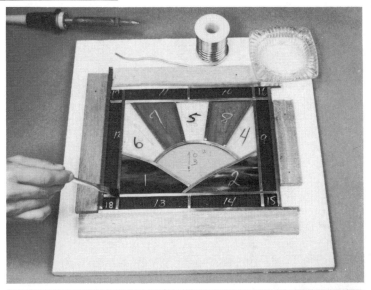

Solder trouble shooting hints:

Symptom	Cure
Solder appears flat—	Add more solder
Solder is rough—	Reflux, remelt solder and pick iron straight up.
Lead is melted—	Iron is too hot or was left on joint too long. Adjust temperature or move iron more swiftly. Reflux, and melt solder into hole.
Joint appears to bulge—	Too much solder. Remelt solder and remove by pulling iron (and molten solder) to the side, then up.
Solder formed into a ball—	Either not enough flux or lead not heated up sufficiently. Reflux, remelt solder, move iron in a circular motion around the joint.

Introduction to Stained Glass

Step 3: After soldering all joints on the top side of the panel, clean it to remove excess flux. You must now turn your panel over. Remove the wooden lath strips and carefully slide the panel to the bench edge. Support the front edge with your hand from underneath and slide the panel over the edge of the bench until you feel it start to fall forward. With your other hand pick up on the back and rotate the panel until it is vertical using the edge of the bench as a fulcrum.

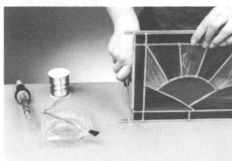

Step 4: Grasp the panel by the top edge and turn it completely around with one edge at the top and the other hand under the bottom and slide the panel down the edge of your bench to the approximate center. Give support to the top edge and roll the panel back onto the workbench.

Step 5: Prepare all joints on this side as previously described in steps 1 & 2 and solder them. To square the corners, cut away the excess perimeter lead. Inspect and clean both sides. Your project is now ready for cementing.

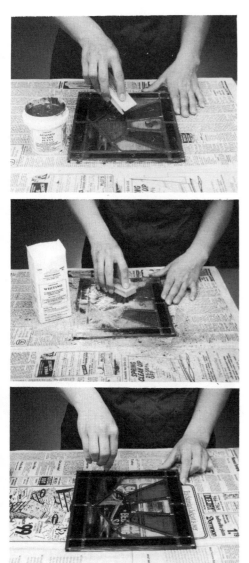

CEMENTING

This is the final stage in completing a leaded panel. Cement must be forced under all lead channels (between the lead and glass) to strengthen and weatherproof the window. This step is necessary even if the window is for an indoor display due to the valuable strength that it adds.

You will require cement, whiting or sawdust, and two natural bristled brushes. (Refer to Page 20 for cementing supplies).

Step 1: Spread some newspaper to cover your work bench and place the panel on it. Gather some cement on the end of the brush and scrub, using a circular motion across each lead channel to deposit the cement.

Step 2: Sprinkle enough whiting onto the panel to lightly cover it. The whiting will soak up the excess oils and helps to dry the cement. Keep the whiting brush flat and scrub vigorously across the leads until all excess cement is removed. Buffing the panel with whiting will darken the lead and solder joints; the longer you scrub the darker they will become. As a side benefit, the abrasive action also cleans and polishes the glass.

Step 3: When the first side is complete, turn your panel over to cement the other side by repeating steps 1 & 2. Leave your panel lying flat for 1 to 3 days to allow the cement to set. During this time some cement may ooze out from under the leads. Remove this excess cement by using a horseshoe nail or a sharpened stick to follow along the leads, around the perimeter of each glass piece.

Note: As an alternative to whiting, sawdust may be used to clean and polish the lead. As a result, the leads will remain shiny until natural oxidation darkens them over a period of months. A polishing wax can be applied to prevent oxidation. (See Page 49, *Polishing* or *Waxing*.)

CHAPTER 7   CONSTRUCTING A COPPER FOIL PANEL

INTRODUCTION

As suggested by its name, copper foil is a thin copper sheet. It is manufactured in tape form with an adhesive back in widths from 1/8" to 1/2". To construct a window using copper foil, the edge of each glass piece is wrapped with the tape. The pieces are then placed on the pattern and soldered together. This method was developed in the late 1800's and used by the Tiffany Company and others to produce intricate lamps and windows.

Occasionally the copper foil method is referred to as "easier than leading for beginners." We feel this is misleading as a *well-made* foil project requires very accurate cutting and soldering skills. The copper foil method is often favored since it can be used to construct almost any project. It allows for great flexibility in design and is structurally rigid while maintaining a delicate appearance.

Copper foil tape is available in widths from 1/8" to 1/2". Generally, the width of foil is matched to the thickness of the glass being wrapped to allow a 1/32" overlap on both top and bottom. The most common sizes used are 3/16", 7/32" and 1/4". Beginning foilers may find the 1/4" width easier to wrap around the glass as centering the glass on the foil is less critical.

Copper foil is available not only in various widths but also in several thicknesses: 1 mil, 1.25 mil and 1.5 mil. The 1 mil foil is the least costly and easiest to fold down but can tear while being applied. The 1.5 mil foil will seldom tear but is more difficult to fold down. Ask your instructor or supplier for their preference.

Step 1: Trace your pattern as described in the section on *Pattern Making* (Page 28-29). Be sure to cut the pattern pieces using the instructions for foil assembly as described on Page 29.

Step 2: Carefully trace the pattern onto the glass using a felt tip pen and cut the glass piece by scoring on the inside of the marker line. *You must always cut the line away* so the marker line is on the waste glass when you break it off. Check your glass piece with the pattern to verify that they are exactly the same size and shape. If the glass is not exact, you must grind it or cut it again. Adjust your cutting to be more precise on the next piece.

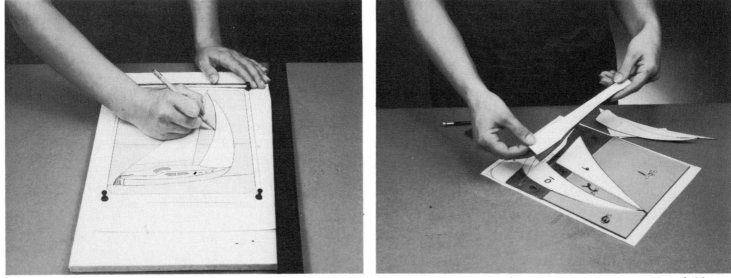

Introduction to Stained Glass

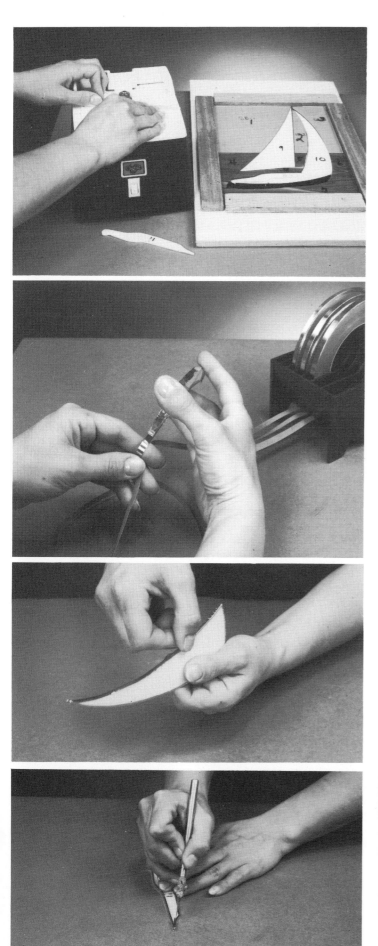

Step 3: When all glass pieces are cut, the next step is to build an assembly jig. To do this, simply nail glazing lath (1/2"x 1" wood trim) along the outside lines of your drawing. Place all the cut glass pieces into your jig. You will find that some pieces require grozing or grinding to make them fit properly. When all pieces fit accurately inside the jig you are ready to wrap with the copper foil. **Note:** If your project is a free-form piece (not a square) secure the glass to the workbench with push pins or horseshoe nails around the outside edge.

Step 4: Clean the cutter lubricant and grinding residue from each piece with glass cleaner before wrapping or the foil will not adhere to the glass easily. Pull a length of foil tape from the roll and peel back several inches of the protective paper backing. Center the glass on the foil leaving the same overhang on either side. Wrap the foil around the entire glass piece, pressing it to the edges with your fingers as you go. Overlap the foil 1/4" at the end and cut it with scissors (or tear it).

Step 5: Fold the foil overhang down onto the glass edge by pinching it with your thumb and index finger. Do this completely around the edge. When folding down an inside curve, press slowly to avoid splitting the foil. If it does split, add a patch long enough to cover the damaged area. Wrap and fold the foil on all glass pieces.

Step 6: The foil overlap must be equal on both sides. If it isn't, the glass wasn't properly centered on the foil. The best solution is to remove the uneven foil and re-wrap the glass with new foil. Some alternatives for a slightly uneven overlap are:
— Trim away too much overlap with an Xacto knife.
— Add a short strip of foil to patch an area with not enough overlap.

Step 7: Use your lathekin as a burnishing tool to press the foil onto all edges until it is smooth and tight against the glass. The foil must be burnished on both sides to ensure it does not pull away from the glass while being soldered.

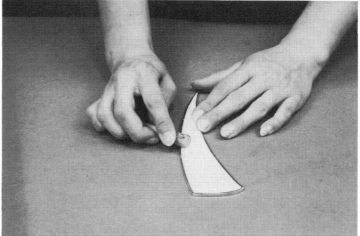

Chapter Seven: Constructing a Copper Foil Panel

SOLDERING COPPER FOIL

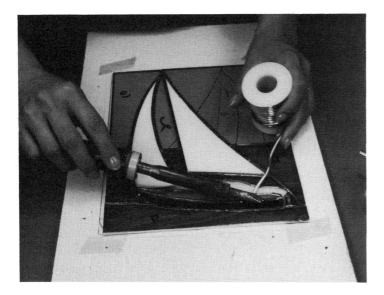

Soldering is the most important step in the copper foil technique because the solder will become the 'lead came,' custom made to fit your project. All exposed copper foil must be soldered (not just the joints), since the foil has no strength without being reinforced with solder.

The solder alloy preferred for copper foil is 60/40 (60% tin and 40% lead). This alloy has favorable melting properties to make copper foil soldering easier.

You will require your soldering iron, solder and flux.

Step 1: Place the foiled glass pieces into the assembly jig. Brush the flux on all the copper foil seams. Rest the *flat* side of the hot soldering iron tip on a seam and melt some solder to coat the foil. Move the iron along the seam, continuously adding more solder, filling the gaps and completely covering the foil as you go. This is referred to as *flat soldering*.

Step 2: Repeat Step 1 with each seam until all are flat soldered. Remove the glazing lath and carefully turn your project over. Apply flux and flat solder the seams, covering all foil on the back side. To prepare for the next step, be sure the panel is turned with the face (front) side up. **Note:** To properly turn a panel over, use the method described on Page 35, Steps 3 and 4.

Step 3: All the flat soldered seams must be built up with more solder until they are rounded and raised. This is called *solder beading*. To run a solder bead, move the iron along a seam while continuously adding solder in a slow uninterrupted motion. If you add sufficient solder and fully heat the seam, the molten solder will flow off the end of your iron into a rounded raised bead. **Note:** When you leave your iron in one area for too long or move the tip along too slowly while beading, the solder previously applied may melt and run through the seam. If this happens, allow that spot to cool, then come back and resolder later.

Step 4: Continue to run a solder bead until all seams on the front side are completed. Depending on the use or method of display, beading may not be required on the back of a panel.

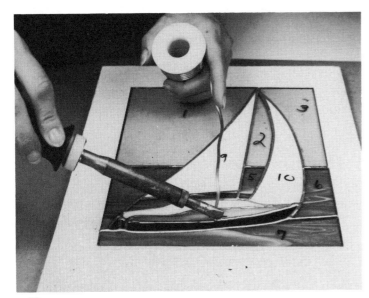

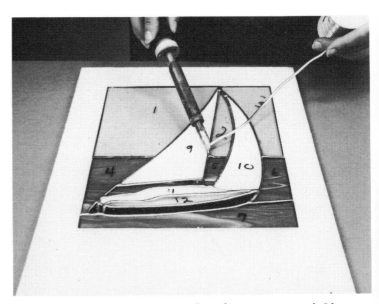

Introduction to Stained Glass

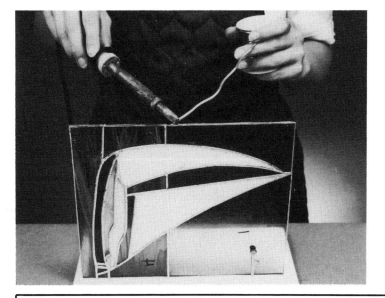

Step 5: All exposed copper foil edges must be *tinned*. This is a light coating of solder that covers the foil. If the panel will be installed in a wood or lead frame (see Page 48), tinning the edge is all that is required. If a frame will not be added, you should bead the outside edges for extra strength and a better appearance. To solder bead an edge, first tin the foil, then stand the panel on its edge and apply molten solder, a little at a time, along the length. Turn the project and repeat for all edges.

Step 6. To hang your panel you must attach wire loops to the top. For instruction and details see page 48, Item 2.

To attach the glass and solder glob details to the sailboat see page 49, Item 7.

Use a glass cleaner to remove flux and solder residue from your project. See page 49, Item 8.

To apply an antique patina to the solder bead (a coppery or black color), see page 48, Item 5.

Solder Trouble-Shooting Hints:

Symptom	Cure
Solder bead appears flat	-Reflux, remelt and add more solder
Rough or uneven bead	-Moving iron too quickly while beading, apply more flux and resolder -Iron might be too cool
Solder will not stick to foil	-Did you apply flux? -Foil may be oxidized and will require buffing with light grade (000) steel wool
Foil is not sticking to the edge of the glass	-Did you clean your glass before foiling? -Were all foil edges pressed tightly to glass (burnished)? -An edge may require a thicker layer of solder to hold the foil in place
Seams are very wide	-Foil is too wide for the thickness of glass being used. -Glass fit was sloppy, leaving large gaps to be filled with solder.
Solder will not flow	-Did you apply flux? -Wrong type of flux -Check iron temperature. It may be too cold.
Solder drips through seam	-Iron is too hot -You are holding iron too long in one spot -May be a large gap between glass pieces. Stick masking tape to the back of this seam to hold drip.
Solder spits and splatters	-Iron too hot -Too much or wrong kind of flux

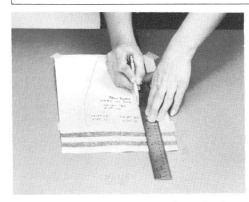

Step 1: Trace pattern as described on Pages 28 & 29, *Pattern Making.*

FIRST— Cut completely around the perimeter (outside) lines of the lamp pattern, following the center of each line.

SECOND— Cut the interior design lines following the center of each line. This will align each section to match the pattern above and below it.

Step 2: Carefully trace the pattern onto the glass using a felt-tip pen and cut the glass piece by scoring on the inside of the marker line. *You must always cut the line away* so the marker line is on the waste glass when you break it off. Check your glass piece with the pattern to verify that they are exactly the same size and shape. If the glass is not exact, you must grind it or cut it. Adjust your scoring to be more precise when scoring the next piece. Continue cutting your glass until all pieces are complete.

NOTE: If you are constructing a lampshade which requires *joiner* glass pieces (see Page 44) DO NOT cut the glass for these pieces.

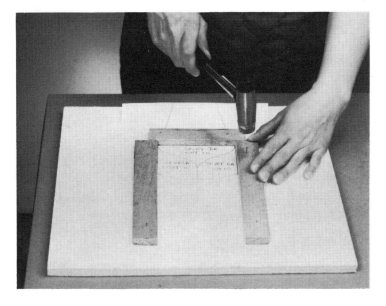

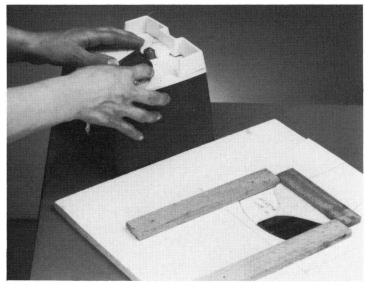

Step 3: When constructing a lamp that has panels with interior designs (a flat section containing two or more pieces), they must be fitted and assembled in a jig. Lay the working drawing (paper copy) of the pattern on your work table, face up. Nail three pieces of glazing lath onto your drawing so the outside line of the section to be assembled is half showing.

Step 4: Place one set of glass pieces into the jig as your drawing shows. If the pieces do not fit accurately, you will have to groze or grind them to fit or cut new ones. When the pieces fit into the jig correctly, clean each piece of glass and copper foil it as described in the *Copper Foil* Section, Pages 36 & 37.

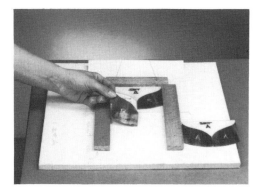

NOTE: If you intend to grind and fit all panel sets before foiling and assembling, you must code each set before removing them from the jig and keep the matched sets together.

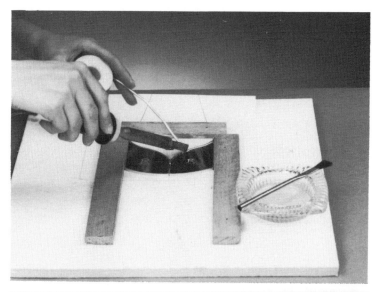

Step 5: Place the foiled glass pieces back into the jig and flat solder them. Remove the panel from the jig, turn it over and flat solder the other side. Finish by running a solder bead on the face side. Repeat for all panels.

Step 6: Start the lamp assembly with the row that is called the main body. This is the large section closest to the vase cap opening. Lay these pieces face side up on the work bench in a semi-circle. Use black plastic electrical tape (or in a pinch, masking tape) and tape the sections together. The areas where tape will come in contact with the glass *must be* clean or the tape will not adhere.

Step 7: Carefully raise this row up into a cone shape, keeping the large diameter end on the bench. Bring the two adjoining side sections together and tape.

Step 8: You must be sure the bottom of the cone is *flat* on the bench. Flux and tack solder each seam at the bottom corner by applying a small dab of molten solder with the tip of your iron.

Step 9: Flux and solder completely around the top opening. Flat solder down the outside of each seam as best you can (leaving tape on) to strengthen the assembly.

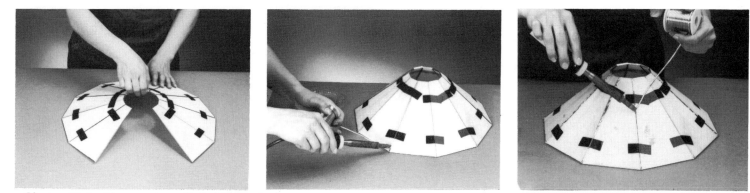

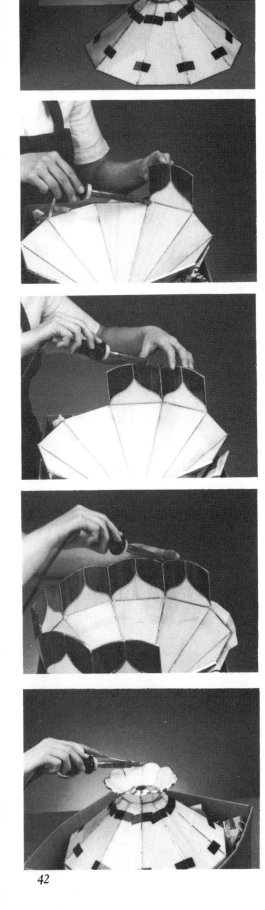

Step 10: *Important Step:* You have probably noticed how flimsy the lamp is at this stage. Attach the vase cap or spider now to strengthen its form. (see *Lamp Hanging Hardware,* Page 46 & 47, Item 1). The bottom must be sitting flat on the table when installing the vase cap to ensure the lamp has a proper shape. When the cap is soldered securely to the outside, carefully turn the lamp over and solder all inside seams and around the vase cap.

Step 11: Place your lamp upside down into a soldering box. (A cardboard box with newspapers loosely crumpled inside.) The assembly will continue by adding the panels of the next row (in the example shown it is the skirt or bottom row). Position and tack solder the first panel of this row to the main body.

Step 12: Place the second panel beside the first and tack it to the main body. Position pieces one and two until the seam meets evenly and tack solder together.

Step 13: Continue by adding the remaining panels in order around the lamp, tacking one to the other as you go. When the complete row is assembled, solder completely around the bottom edge. For more strength and stability, flat solder all the inside seams before moving on.

Step 14: Turn the lamp right side up in the soldering box. If you are constructing a lamp with a crown (upper most row) use the same procedure as described for the skirt assembly in Step 11, 12 & 13.

Step 15: The lamp should be completely assembled now and ready for final soldering. Remove all remaining tape. Position the lamp in the soldering box and level the seam you intend to solder (horizontal to the floor). Take your time and run a bead of solder. If the molten solder is flowing away from the seam or appears to be running downhill, this indicates the seam is not perfectly level. Reposition the lamp in the box and resume soldering.

HINT: If you are trying to fill a gap (a space between two foiled pieces), and the molten solder falls through, cover the space from the inside with masking tape to keep the solder from dripping.

Step 16: When you have completed soldering, do a quality check of all seams inside and out to make sure they are finished and uniform. Fine bead soldering is a difficult skill to master, don't be discouraged, remember practice makes perfect.

To finish your lamp, solder a wire around the bottom edge. For instruction and details see Page 48, Item 4.

To clean your project of flux and solder residue use a glass cleaner, see Page 49, Item 8.

To apply an antique patina to the solder beads (a coppery or black color), see Page 48, Item 5.

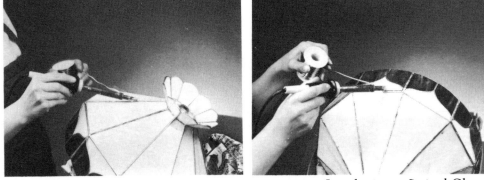

Introduction to Stained Glass

Instead of the row assembly described earlier, an alternative used by many crafters is a system called *row on row* assembly.

To use this method, substitute steps 11, 12, 13, & 14 in lamp assembly description.

Step 11: Place your lamp upside down into a soldering box. (A cardboard box with newspapers loosely crumpled inside as shown). The assembly will continue by adding the panels of the next row (in the example shown it is the skirt or bottom row). Lay these panels in sequence, side by side and face up on your bench. Tape them together in the same manner as you taped the main body. Gently lift the row on its edge, bend it around into a circle and tape the ends together. Tack solder all seams at top and bottom corners only.

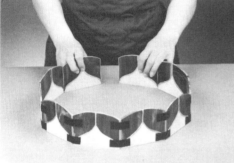

Step 12: Turn the main body section upside down into the soldering box. Gently lift the skirt section and place it on the main body. The seam corners of the two sections must line up one to the other. Tack solder the sections together at these corners.

Step 13: When the complete row is attached, solder completely around the bottom edge. For more strength and stability, flat solder all the inside seams before moving on.

Step 14: Turn the lamp right side up in the soldering box. If you are constructing a lamp with a crown (upper most row) use the same procedure as for the skirt assembly in Steps 11, 12, & 13.

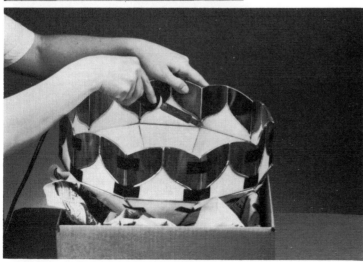

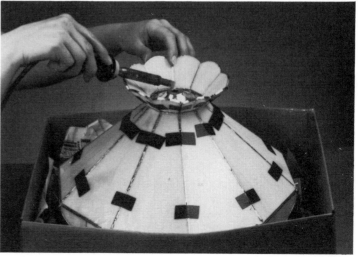

Chapter Eight: Constructing a Foiled Lampshade

SPECIAL CONSTRUCTION

JOINER PIECES

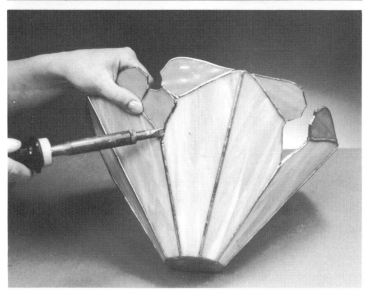

Some lampshades must have glass (joiner) pieces inserted to join the sections once the shade has been assembled. A joiner piece usually bridges a gap between two sections which are at an angle. (See Floral Lamp, project 12 for an example.)

Step 1: Place the pattern for the joiner piece in the appropriate space to see if the size is satisfactory. If the pattern correctly fits the space, cut out the glass piece.

Step 2: If the fit is unsatisfactory you must make a new pattern of the space by placing a piece of pattern card underneath the hole and tracing around it with a marking pen. Cut the glass for the joiner piece according to this new pattern.
NOTE: Verify the size of each space individually with the pattern before cutting the glass.

Step 3: Fit the glass piece into its designated space by grinding or grozing as necessary. Wrap the piece with copper foil. Insert it into the space so the edges are flush with the adjacent sections and tack solder it. Do not be too concerned if all edges are not completely flush since that is virtually impossible.

Step 4: Verify the pattern for the next joiner piece and cut the glass piece. Wrap it with copper foil, insert into place and tack solder it. Repeat this procedure for each joiner piece until all are installed. Finish the seams with a solder bead.

Introduction to Stained Glass

A project that contains 90° corners (such as a box) must be assembled correctly to give the corners proper strength. You must use the method described to construct projects #13 & #14 in this book.

Step 1: Have the bottom and all side glass pieces cut and wrapped with copper foil. Begin assembly by holding two side pieces together with a 90° corner. The corner must meet edge-to-edge as shown in the photo. (A butt end construction is not recommended.)

Step 2: Tack solder the side pieces together at the top and bottom of the corner seam. Repeat this procedure to attach the remaining sides.

Step 3: Carefully place the bottom on the box sides. It should sit on the inside edges of the side pieces. Occasionally the bottom will fall through, if this happens place a strip of paper across the sides to hold the bottom up.

Step 4: Tack solder the bottom to the sides at the corners. Flat solder around the bottom seams, turn the box over and solder the inside seams. Finish all seams and edges with a solder bead and clean.

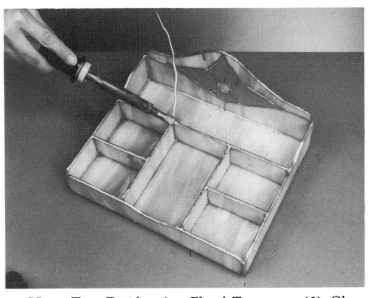

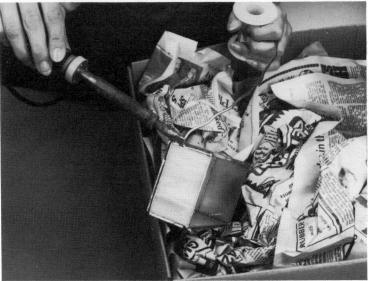

Note: Tray Dividers (see Floral Tray, page 62): Glass pieces used to section off a tray (or box bottom) are inserted after the tray is assembled. First wrap the pieces and tin all edges. Position them in the tray as the pattern indicates and tack solder at all seams top and bottom.

HANGING HARDWARE

1. Lamp Hanging Hardware: This is an integral part of a lampshade. It must be securely soldered to the top opening of a lampshade to solidify the structure and to provide hanging support for the electrical hardware. There are many different types of hanging hardware available, we will describe the two most common:

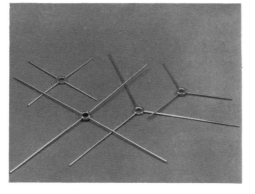

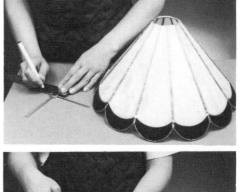

Spider

This is a brass ring about one inch in diameter with 3 or 4 arms radiating out from 6" to 12". The number of arms must divide evenly into the number of sides of your shade. For example, a six-sided shade requires a 3 arm spider while an eight-sided shade requires a 4 arm spider.

Installation:

Step 1: To ensure the spider hole is centered, measure the top opening of your lampshade and divide this dimension by two. For example, a 4" opening divided by two is 2". Measure this distance from the center of the spider's central-hole down an arm and mark with a pen. Measure and mark all arms.

Step 2: Use a pair of pliers to bend the arms down at the marks. The angle of the bend must match the top angle of the lampshade. The first trial bend is simply a guess at the correct angle.

Step 3: Gently turn the lamp upside down and test the arm angles by positioning and centering the spider in the shade opening. Adjust the angles as needed. Each arm should extend approximately two to four inches from the top of the opening and straight down each seam, cut them shorter if necessary.

Step 4: When the spider fits the opening correctly, remove and tin each arm from the bend to the outside tip. Position and center the spider into the shade opening and solder the arms securely down the inside seams.

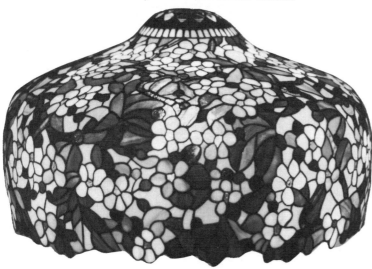

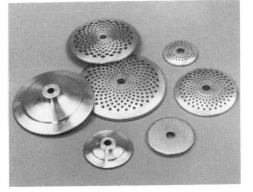

These are brass (or copper) disks which are available in various sizes. They can be plain or ventilated with fancy designs. The size must be matched to the shade top diameter.

INSTALLATION:

Step 1: To install a cap properly it should fit just inside the shade opening. This will ensure that it is soldered securely to the vertical seams of the lampshade. Vase caps are manufactured in standard sizes and often the shade opening is an odd size. Most vase caps can be cut down with sheet metal shears to custom fit the opening.

Step 2: If you were unable to find a cap to fit the shade opening exactly, choose a cap which is slightly larger than the opening. To mark the cap for trimming, place it on the shade opening from the outside and use a felt-tip pen to trace around the opening from the inside.

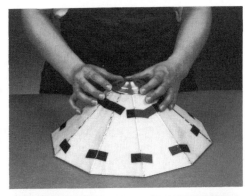

Step 3: Trim the cap following the traced line with sheet metal shears (tin snips). Place the cap back on the shade to check the fit and adjust as necessary.

Step 4: The outside surface of the vase cap should be *tinned* with a thin layer of solder before installation. Tinning will allow antique patina (see Page 48, Item 5) to color the cap the same as the rest of the solder seams. It will also make soldering the cap to the shade easier.

NOTE: Since the vase cap draws heat away from the soldering area (referred to as heatsinking) it is more difficult to make the solder flow. To ensure a smooth finish, more time will be required to heat both solder and metal while tinning.

Step 5: Position the cap on the shade opening and tack solder it. The cap must be centered and level on the shade. When the fit is correct, solder fully around the cap inside and out.

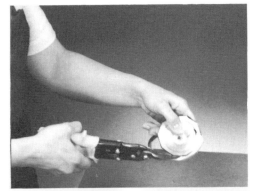

Note: If you are constructing a large shade, you can combine a cap and a spider for added strength.

WARNING: When wiring and installing your lamp you must consider all federal and local electrical codes and regulations.

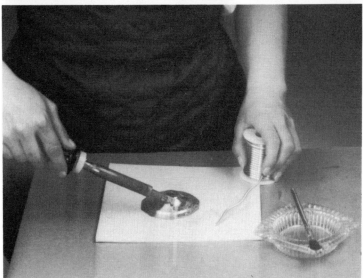

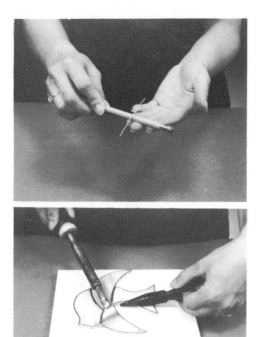

2. Window Hanging Hardware

To suspend a panel or a suncatcher you must attach wire rings to the top edge. Make a loop from brass or copper wire (12-18) by wrapping it around a pencil. Leave the ends long enough so they can be soldered down a lead or foil seam. If the wire is attached only at an edge, where there is no seam, it will pull the foil or lead from the glass.

When the loop has been cut and shaped, hold it with a pair of needle nose pliers, first tin it, then position the wire and solder into place.

3. Frames for Copper Foil Panels

U or H shaped lead came, cut and attached to the outside edge of a copper foiled panel, will make a satisfactory frame. An allowance must be made for the depth of the channel by removing a small amount of the solder bead at the edge (or by not beading out to the edge).

Step 1: Cut the came to fit around the outside edges. If the panel is square, measure and cut the four pieces and miter (a 45° angle) the corners. If it is round, wrap a single piece of came around the perimeter and butt the ends together.

Step 2: Place the panel on your work table. Fit the came on the edges and secure with horseshoe nails. Solder the came at the corners and to all the copper foil seams. Remove the horseshoe nails, carefully turn the panel over (see page 35) and solder.

Step 3: Solder a loop into the corners for hanging as described previously in Item 2. For a more rigid frame, zinc, brass or copper came can be substituted for the lead.

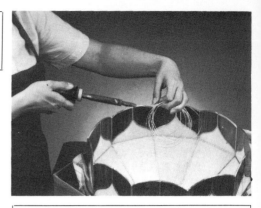

4. Wire support around bottom of lamp

It is recommended that a wire (14-18 gauge, brass or copper) be soldered around the bottom edge of your lamp for reinforcement. The wire will help to finish the bottom edge and holds it firmly together. Tack solder one piece of wire completely around the bottom edge and overlap the ends at least ½ inch. Finish the edge with a solder bead.

5. Antique Patina

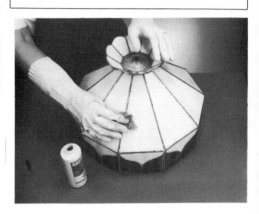

Best results are achieved when patina is applied to solder immediately after it is completed and cleaned with glass cleaner. Rub the solder using a soft rag or brush soaked with the liquid patina. Clean the solution from the glass immediately. Wear rubber gloves while handling this solution.

If your project has been finished for a few days, you must scrub down all the soldered seams with fine steel wool or a metal pot scrubber and clean to remove all corrosion before applying the patina.

6. Polishing or Waxing

To preserve the shiny finish on the solder after a patina has been applied, use a good quality spray furniture polish. Apply the polish and rub all solder seams vigorously. For an even shinier finish, polish the patina with a jeweler's rouge cloth or use a brass or silver polish. Finish with an application of car wax. You can even polish the wax with a power car polisher. Wax can be used to preserve the shiny finish leads after cementing and cleaning with sawdust.

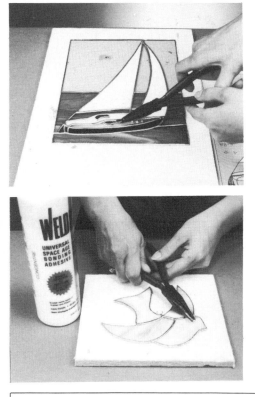

7. Overlay Details

Some projects call for details such as eyes, mouth, nose, etc. which are formed using solder or wire and require glue to fasten them in place. Some adhesives that can be used are clear silicone seal, white bond glue or epoxy.

Brass Filigree— There are many designs of brass filigree available to decorate your project. This is simply a thin brass sheet which has been punched with a design. To use them you must first tin the top surface by applying a thin coat of molten solder. When cool, clean both sides, position and solder it around the edge to secure it to a seam.

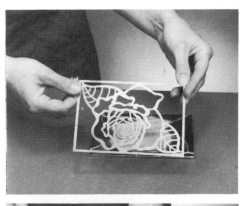

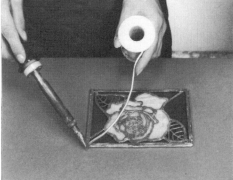

8. CLEANING YOUR PROJECT

It is very important to clean your project as soon as you have finished working on it. If the flux is left on, it will corrode the lead and solder even overnight. This will make touch-up soldering or final clean-up difficult. Any good quality glass cleaner will work, as will a solution of vinegar and water.

If the solder or lead has corroded and is difficult to solder they can be cleaned by scrubbing with fine steel wool or a small wire brush. **Caution:** If you have already applied antique patina to the solder, scrubbing will remove it.

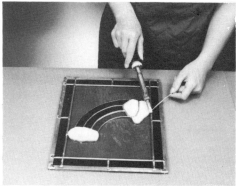

Glass Overlays— An effective and easy way to decorate a mirror or a window is to add a suncatcher overlay to a corner. Construct both items separately and clean thoroughly. Position and solder the overlay to the host panel. If there are only a few joints to attach with solder, glue it as well.

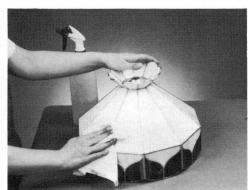

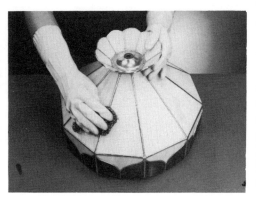

9. REINFORCING YOUR WINDOW

A large window, once installed, will bow or sag under its own weight if not reinforced properly with steel bars. The traditional method is to fasten round steel bars to the window by tying them with copper wire that has been soldered to the leads. A more recent method is to use a flat steel bar which can be bent to follow a lead or soldered foil seam from one edge to the other. This bar is usually made from steel, galvanized (coated) with tin so that it can be soldered directly to the seam it is following. The ends of the bar should be attached to the window frame during installation.

If you intend to construct a window 6 square feet or larger, especially if it is to be installed in a door, you will need to consider reinforcing it. If in doubt ask your instructor or supplier for advice.

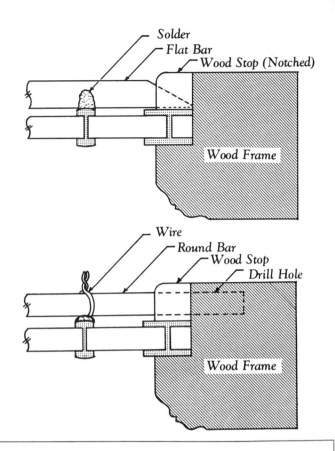

Solder
Flat Bar
Wood Stop (Notched)
Wood Frame

Wire
Round Bar
Wood Stop
Drill Hole
Wood Frame

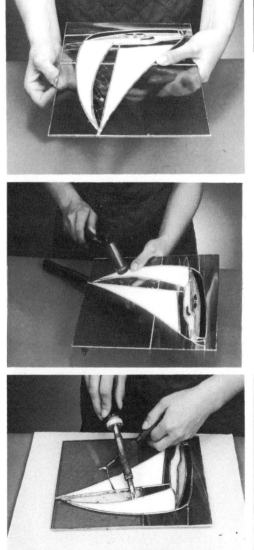

REPLACING A CRACKED FOIL PIECE

In the event that a glass piece cracks after a panel (or lamp) has been soldered, it is a relatively easy procedure to replace it. **Caution!** You must wear safety glasses while removing the broken glass piece.

Step 1: Make several scores on the surface of the cracked glass piece from edge to edge. Tap the back with the ball end of your cutter to crack the scores.

Step 2: Use two hammers (or a hammer and heavy pliers). Hold one on the underside of the cracked piece and tap with the other on the topside until the pieces break out.

Step 3: Flux and melt the solder away until you can grip the old foil with a pair of needle nose pliers. As you melt the solder, *gently* pull on the foil until it has been completely removed. Move your iron around the edge to smooth off the excess solder.

Step 4: Make a pattern of the space by placing a piece of pattern card underneath the hole and trace around it with a marking pen.

Step 5: Cut out the new glass piece according to your pattern. Fit it into the space, grind or groze if needed, and wrap it with copper foil. Position and tack solder it into place and complete with a solder bead. Clean the glass and patina the solder if required.

50

Introduction to Stained Glass

CHAPTER TEN
FULL-SIZE PROJECT PATTERNS

The importance of using an accurate pattern cannot be stressed enough. You should consider the following points when copying and cutting your pattern.

—Trace and cut the patterns down the middle of the printed line except when cutting for lead assembly, when you should remove the line.

—When the pattern instructions read "Cut 1 up/Cut 1 down" (see project **8**) cut a glass piece with the pattern face side up then flip it over (face side down) and cut a glass piece.

—The degree of difficulty is intended to be used as a guide only. A "1" is a beginner level and would be suitable as a first project. A "5" is an intermediate project and should not be attempted until you have constructed a few items to sufficiently develop your skills.

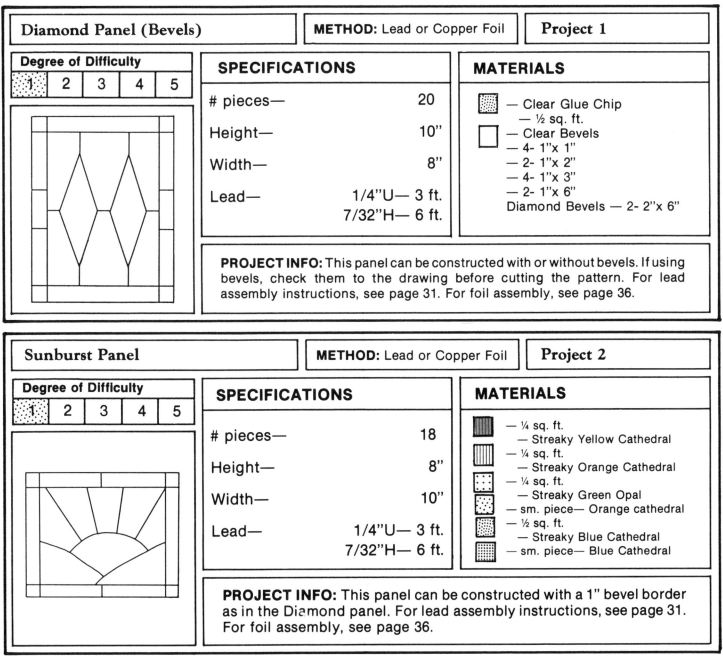

Diamond Panel (Bevels)	METHOD: Lead or Copper Foil	Project 1

Degree of Difficulty

1	2	3	4	5

SPECIFICATIONS

# pieces—	20
Height—	10"
Width—	8"
Lead—	1/4"U— 3 ft.
	7/32"H— 6 ft.

MATERIALS

— Clear Glue Chip
— ½ sq. ft.
— Clear Bevels
— 4- 1"x 1"
— 2- 1"x 2"
— 4- 1"x 3"
— 2- 1"x 6"
Diamond Bevels — 2- 2"x 6"

PROJECT INFO: This panel can be constructed with or without bevels. If using bevels, check them to the drawing before cutting the pattern. For lead assembly instructions, see page 31. For foil assembly, see page 36.

Sunburst Panel	METHOD: Lead or Copper Foil	Project 2

Degree of Difficulty

1	2	3	4	5

SPECIFICATIONS

# pieces—	18
Height—	8"
Width—	10"
Lead—	1/4"U— 3 ft.
	7/32"H— 6 ft.

MATERIALS

— ¼ sq. ft.
— Streaky Yellow Cathedral
— ¼ sq. ft.
— Streaky Orange Cathedral
— ¼ sq. ft.
— Streaky Green Opal
— sm. piece— Orange cathedral
— ½ sq. ft.
— Streaky Blue Cathedral
— sm. piece— Blue Cathedral

PROJECT INFO: This panel can be constructed with a 1" bevel border as in the Diamond panel. For lead assembly instructions, see page 31. For foil assembly, see page 36.

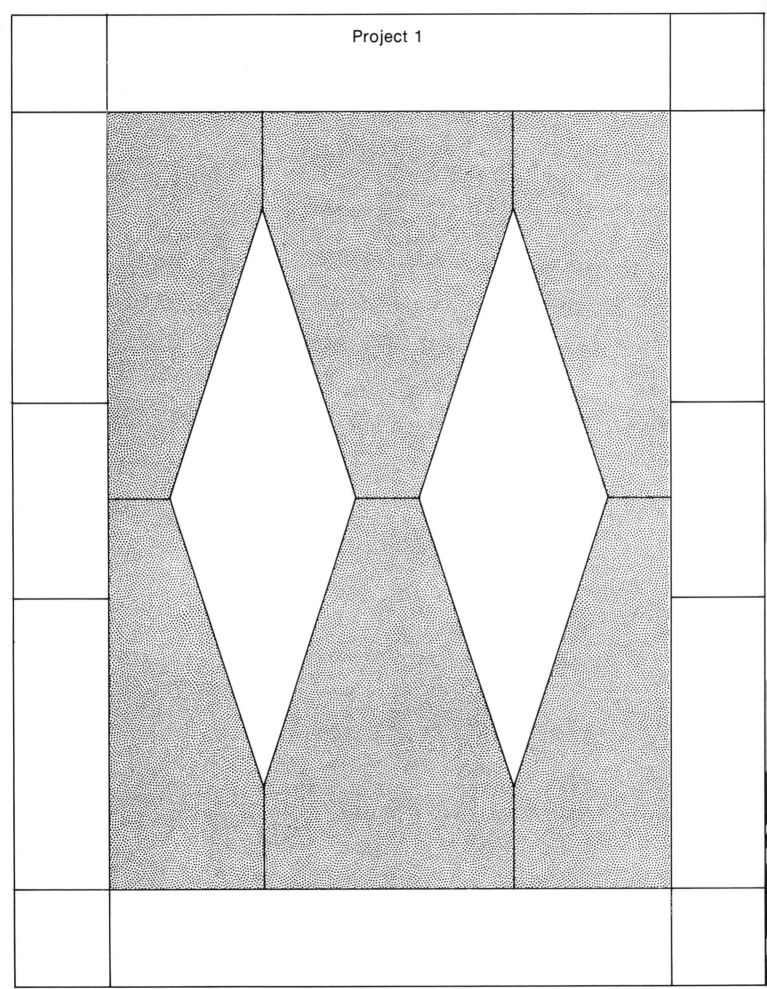

Introduction to Stained Glass

Project 2

Butterfly	METHOD: Copper Foil	Project 3

Degree of Difficulty

1	2	3	4	5

SPECIFICATIONS

pieces—   5

Height—   7"

Width—   4"

MATERIALS

▓ — small piece
— Dk. Blue Cath.

▒ — ½ sq. ft.
— Strky. Blue/Yellow
Cathedral

PROJECT INFO: Butterfly antennas and legs are made from 18 gauge wire and soldered into place. The dash line ----- indicates placement for soldering the hanging loop/reinforcing wire.

Rainbow & Cloud	METHOD: Copper Foil	Project 4

Degree of Difficulty

1	2	3	4	5

SPECIFICATIONS

pieces—   6

Height—   4"

Width—   9"

MATERIALS

☐ — ¼ sq. ft.
— Streaky White Opal
▓ — small piece
— Cathedral Blue
▤ — small piece
— Cathedral Red
▥ — small piece
— Cathedral Yellow

PROJECT INFO: To properly support this suncatcher, the hanging wire must be soldered along the top edge and into the foil seams as indicated by the dash line ---. This project can also be used as a panel overlay as it is shown in the color photographs.

Standing Angel	METHOD: Copper Foil	Project 5

Degree of Difficulty

1	2	3	4	5

SPECIFICATIONS

pieces—   5

Height—   6½"

MATERIALS

▥ — ¼ sq. ft.
— Light Mauve Opal
▒ — ¼ sq. ft.
— Strky. White Opal
☐ — White - Jewel or Glob

PROJECT INFO: This angel's head can be a white nugget (as ours is); it can be a faceted oval jewel or you could cut it from a piece of glass. **To assemble:** Stand the two body pieces on end (90⁰) and tack solder top and bottom. Position the head and tack solder it to the body. The arms are made from wire and the hymn book is flattened lead.

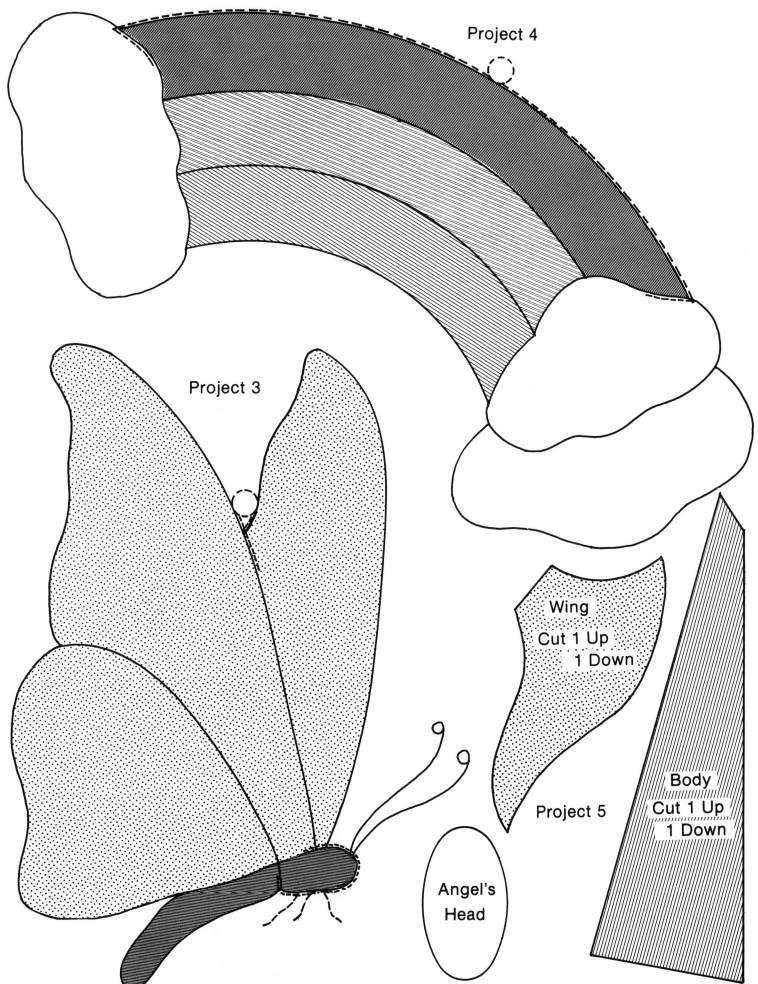

Project 4

Project 3

Wing
Cut 1 Up
1 Down

Project 5

Angel's
Head

Body
Cut 1 Up
1 Down

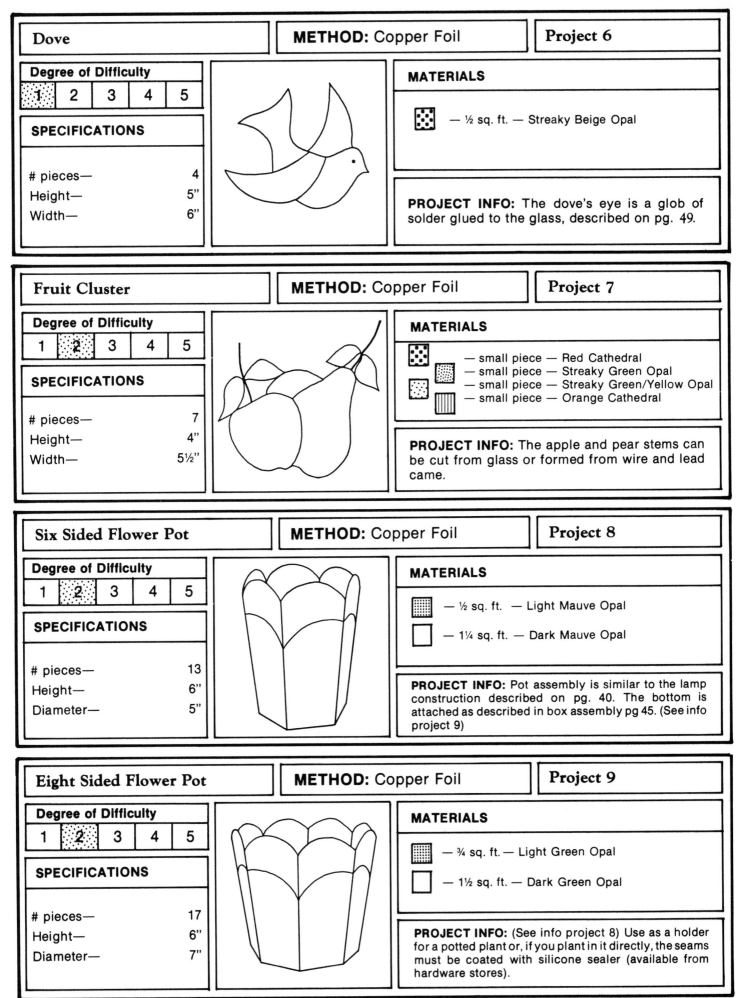

Dove   **METHOD:** Copper Foil   **Project 6**

Degree of Difficulty

| 1 | 2 | 3 | 4 | 5 |

SPECIFICATIONS

# pieces—	4
Height—	5"
Width—	6"

MATERIALS

— ½ sq. ft. — Streaky Beige Opal

PROJECT INFO: The dove's eye is a glob of solder glued to the glass, described on pg. 49.

Fruit Cluster   **METHOD:** Copper Foil   **Project 7**

Degree of Difficulty

| 1 | 2 | 3 | 4 | 5 |

SPECIFICATIONS

# pieces—	7
Height—	4"
Width—	5½"

MATERIALS

— small piece — Red Cathedral
— small piece — Streaky Green Opal
— small piece — Streaky Green/Yellow Opal
— small piece — Orange Cathedral

PROJECT INFO: The apple and pear stems can be cut from glass or formed from wire and lead came.

Six Sided Flower Pot   **METHOD:** Copper Foil   **Project 8**

Degree of Difficulty

| 1 | 2 | 3 | 4 | 5 |

SPECIFICATIONS

# pieces—	13
Height—	6"
Diameter—	5"

MATERIALS

— ½ sq. ft. — Light Mauve Opal
— 1¼ sq. ft. — Dark Mauve Opal

PROJECT INFO: Pot assembly is similar to the lamp construction described on pg. 40. The bottom is attached as described in box assembly pg 45. (See info project 9)

Eight Sided Flower Pot   **METHOD:** Copper Foil   **Project 9**

Degree of Difficulty

| 1 | 2 | 3 | 4 | 5 |

SPECIFICATIONS

# pieces—	17
Height—	6"
Diameter—	7"

MATERIALS

— ¾ sq. ft. — Light Green Opal
— 1½ sq. ft. — Dark Green Opal

PROJECT INFO: (See info project 8) Use as a holder for a potted plant or, if you plant in it directly, the seams must be coated with silicone sealer (available from hardware stores).

Project 6

Project 7

Project 8 & 9

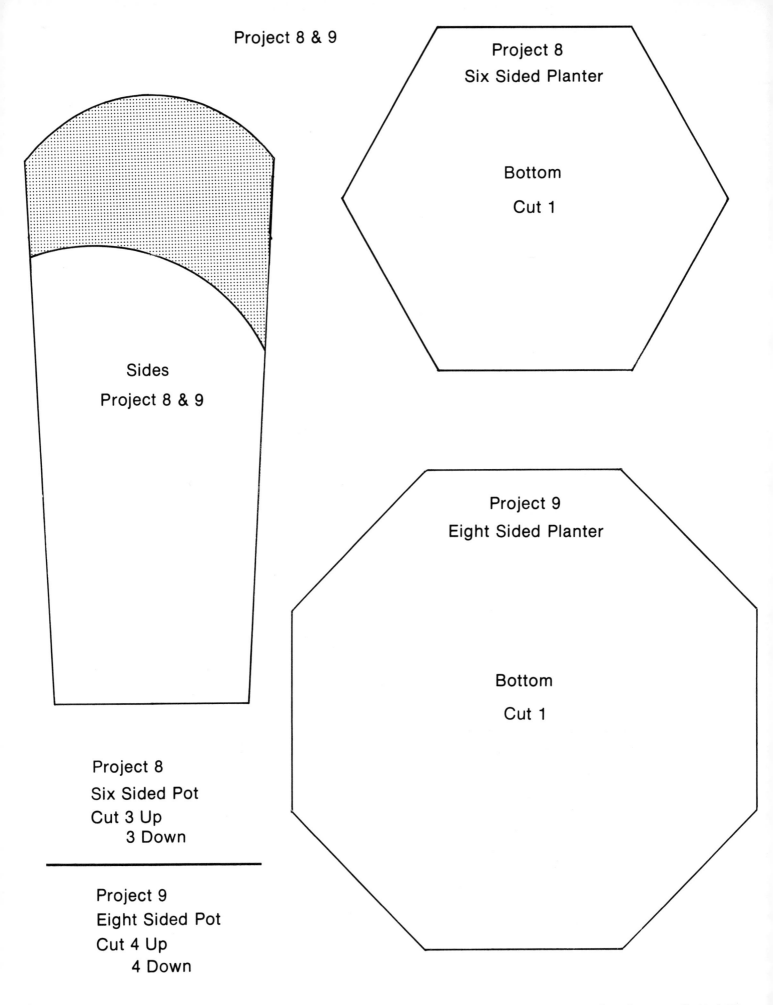

Project 8
Six Sided Planter

Bottom

Cut 1

Sides
Project 8 & 9

Project 9
Eight Sided Planter

Bottom

Cut 1

Project 8

Six Sided Pot
Cut 3 Up
    3 Down

Project 9
Eight Sided Pot
Cut 4 Up
    4 Down

Introduction to Stained Glass

Traditional Cone Lamp

METHOD: Copper Foil   **Project 10**

Degree of Difficulty

1	2	3	4	5

SPECIFICATIONS

# pieces—	24
Sides—	12
Height—	7½"
Bottom Diameter—	13½"
Top Diameter—	2¼"

MATERIALS

☐ — 2 sq. ft.
   — Light Mauve Opal
▨ — ½ sq. ft.
   — Dark Mauve Cathedral or Glue Chip

PROJECT INFO: As an option, the bottom trim band can be left off to create an easily and quickly constructed lampshade. For assembly instructions see pg. 40.

Classic Lamp

METHOD: Copper Foil   **Project 11**

Degree of Difficulty

1	2	3	4	5

SPECIFICATIONS

# pieces—	50
Sides—	10
Height—	9½"
Bottom Diameter—	13½"
Top Diameter—	2¾"

MATERIALS

☐ — 3½ sq. ft.
   — Beige Opal
▨ — 1 sq. ft.
   — Streaky Brown Opal

PROJECT INFO: The skirt design is provided with several options (see color photos) choose the style you want and follow the correct dash or solid lines to trace and cut your pattern. For assembly instructions see pg. 40

Floral Lamp

METHOD: Copper Foil   **Project 12**

Degree of Difficulty

1	2	3	4	5

SPECIFICATIONS

# pieces—	45
Sides—	10
Height—	9"
Bottom Diameter—	12½"
Top Diameter—	2¾"

MATERIALS

☐ — 3 sq. ft.
   — Light Green Opal
▨ — 1 sq. ft.
   — Pink Opal
▨ —small piece
   — Yellow Opal

PROJECT INFO: Read the section on joiner pieces (pg. 44) before cutting the glass for this project. For assembly instructions see pg. 40.

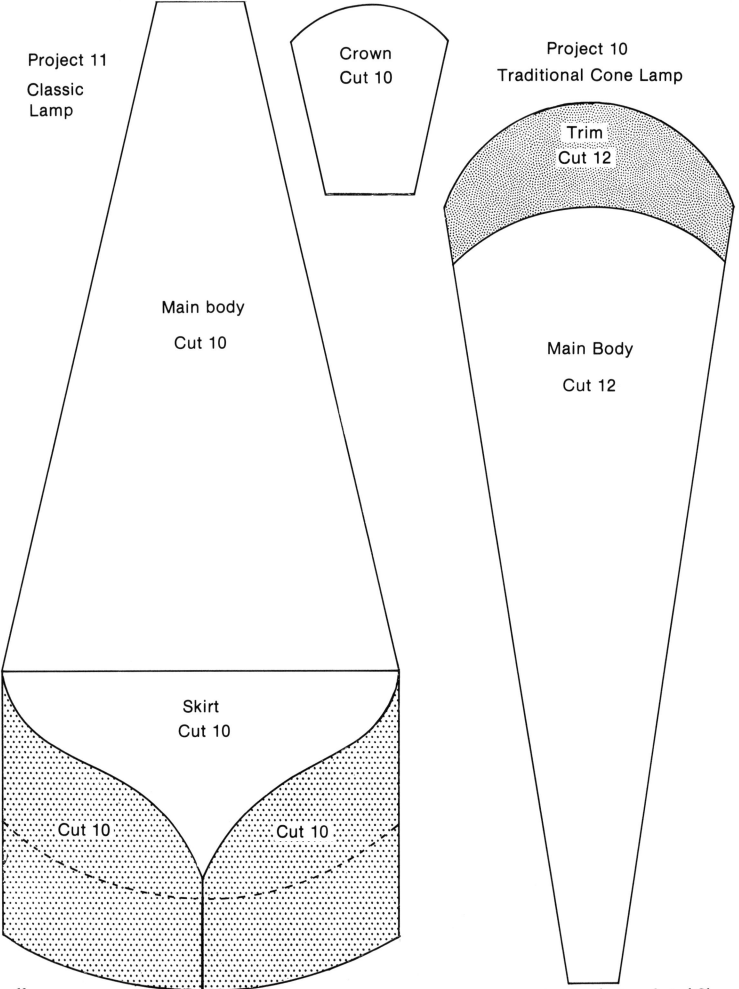

Project 11

Classic
Lamp

Crown
Cut 10

Project 10

Traditional Cone Lamp

Trim
Cut 12

Main body

Cut 10

Main Body

Cut 12

Skirt
Cut 10

Cut 10

Cut 10

Project 12   Floral Lamp

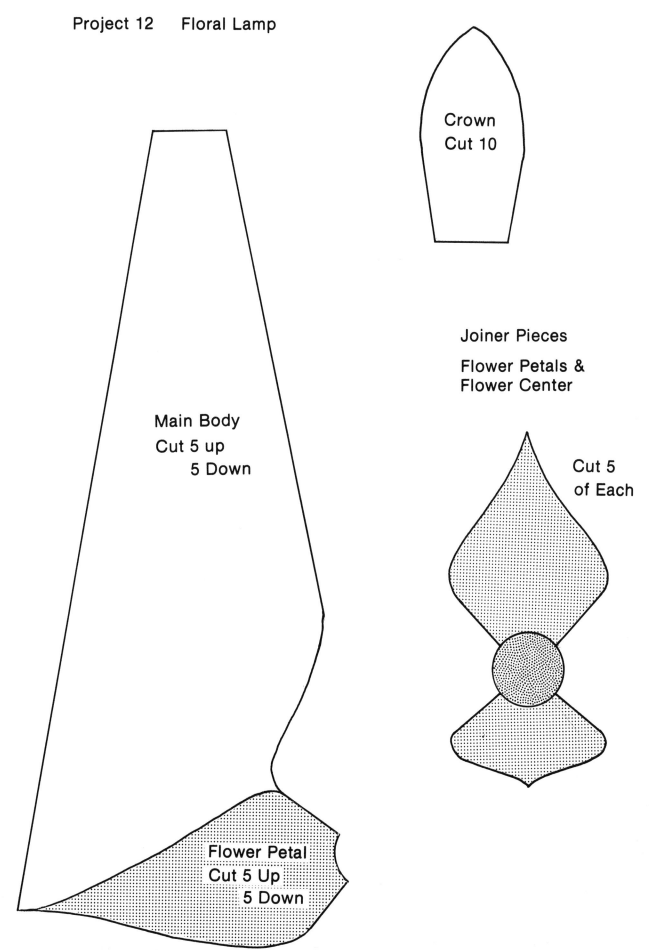

Crown
Cut 10

Joiner Pieces

Flower Petals &
Flower Center

Cut 5
of Each

Main Body
Cut 5 up
    5 Down

Flower Petal
Cut 5 Up
    5 Down

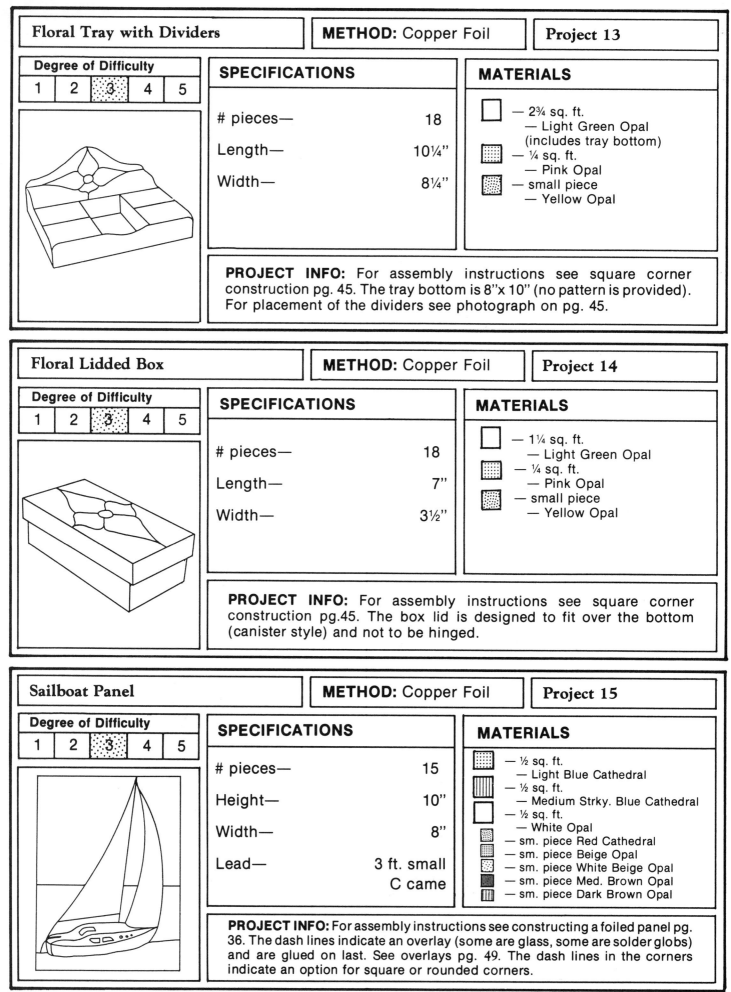

Floral Tray with Dividers

METHOD: Copper Foil   **Project 13**

Degree of Difficulty
1	2	3	4	5

SPECIFICATIONS
# pieces—	18
Length—	10¼"
Width—	8¼"

MATERIALS
- ☐ — 2¾ sq. ft.
  — Light Green Opal (includes tray bottom)
- ▦ — ¼ sq. ft.
  — Pink Opal
- ▨ — small piece
  — Yellow Opal

PROJECT INFO: For assembly instructions see square corner construction pg. 45. The tray bottom is 8"x 10" (no pattern is provided). For placement of the dividers see photograph on pg. 45.

Floral Lidded Box

METHOD: Copper Foil   **Project 14**

Degree of Difficulty
1	2	3	4	5

SPECIFICATIONS
# pieces—	18
Length—	7"
Width—	3½"

MATERIALS
- ☐ — 1¼ sq. ft.
  — Light Green Opal
- ▦ — ¼ sq. ft.
  — Pink Opal
- ▨ — small piece
  — Yellow Opal

PROJECT INFO: For assembly instructions see square corner construction pg.45. The box lid is designed to fit over the bottom (canister style) and not to be hinged.

Sailboat Panel

METHOD: Copper Foil   **Project 15**

Degree of Difficulty
1	2	3	4	5

SPECIFICATIONS
# pieces—	15
Height—	10"
Width—	8"
Lead—	3 ft. small C came

MATERIALS
- ▦ — ½ sq. ft.
  — Light Blue Cathedral
- ▥ — ½ sq. ft.
  — Medium Strky. Blue Cathedral
- ☐ — ½ sq. ft.
  — White Opal
- ▨ — sm. piece Red Cathedral
- ▨ — sm. piece Beige Opal
- ▨ — sm. piece White Beige Opal
- ▨ — sm. piece Med. Brown Opal
- ▥ — sm. piece Dark Brown Opal

PROJECT INFO: For assembly instructions see constructing a foiled panel pg. 36. The dash lines indicate an overlay (some are glass, some are solder globs) and are glued on last. See overlays pg. 49. The dash lines in the corners indicate an option for square or rounded corners.

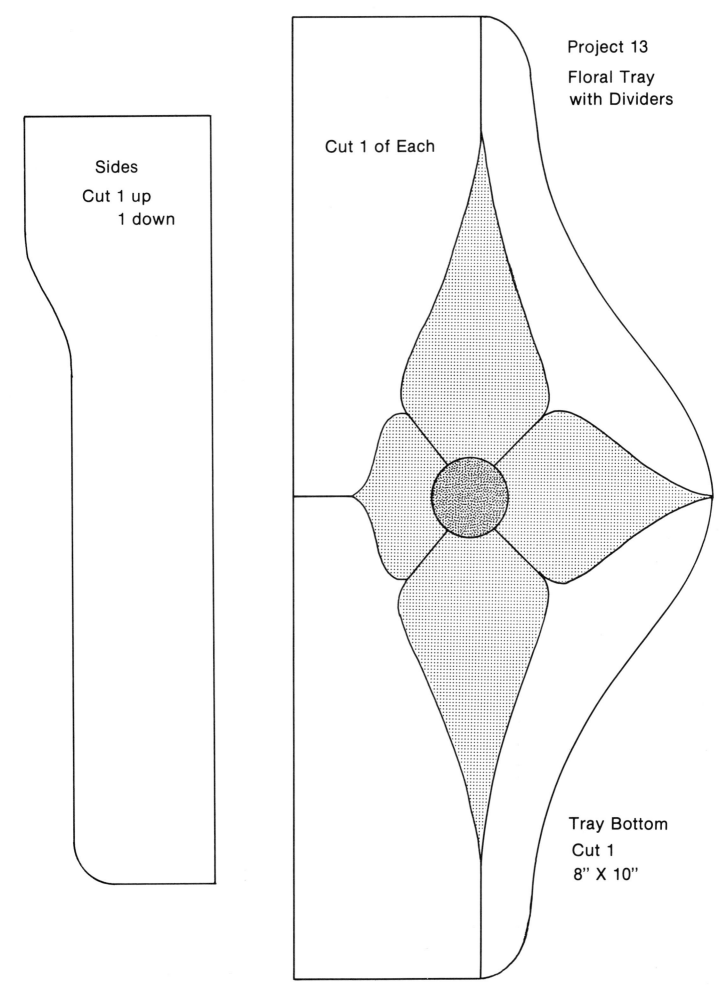

Sides
Cut 1 up
1 down

Project 13
Floral Tray
with Dividers

Cut 1 of Each

Tray Bottom
Cut 1
8" X 10"

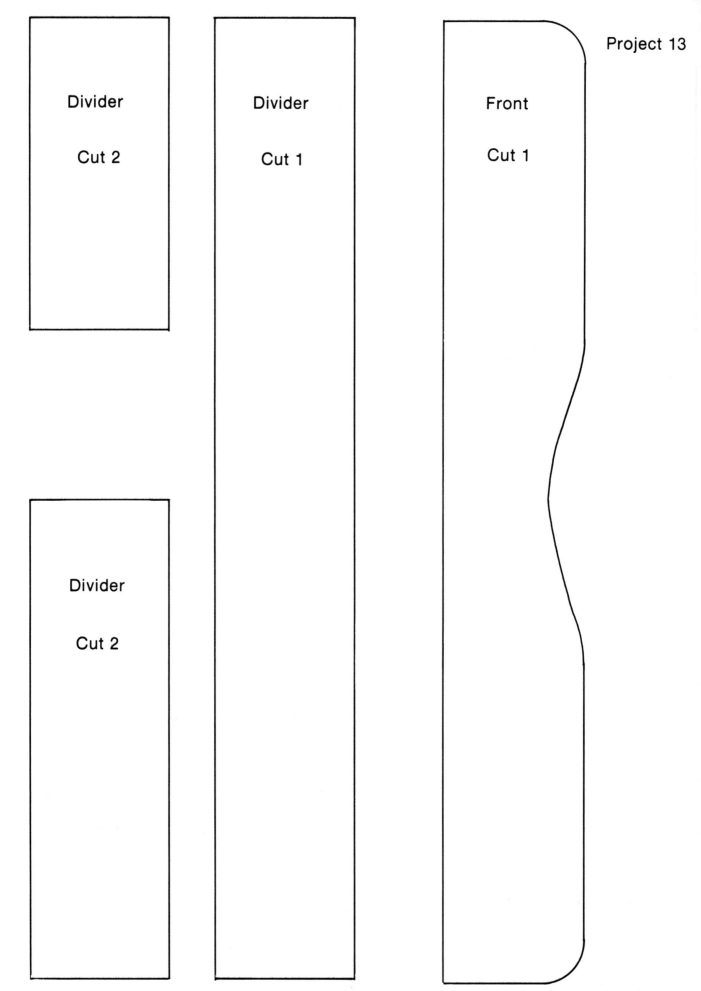

Divider

Cut 2

Divider

Cut 1

Front

Cut 1

Divider

Cut 2

Introduction to Stained Glass

Project 14   Floral Lidded Box

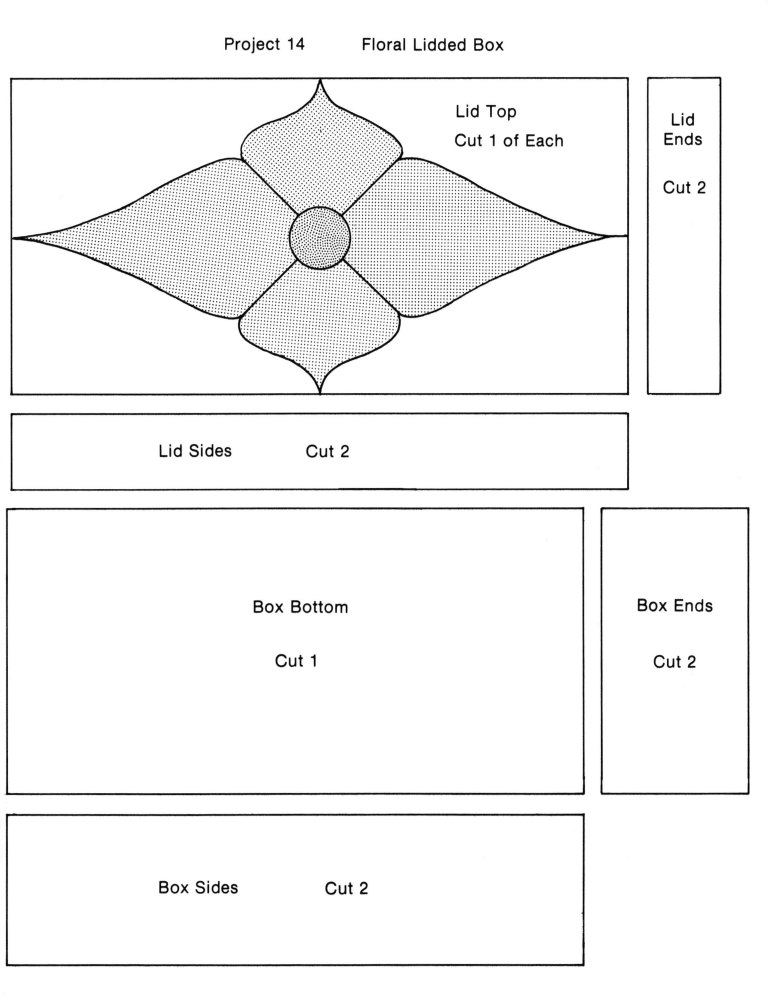

Lid Top
Cut 1 of Each

Lid Ends
Cut 2

Lid Sides   Cut 2

Box Bottom

Cut 1

Box Ends

Cut 2

Box Sides   Cut 2

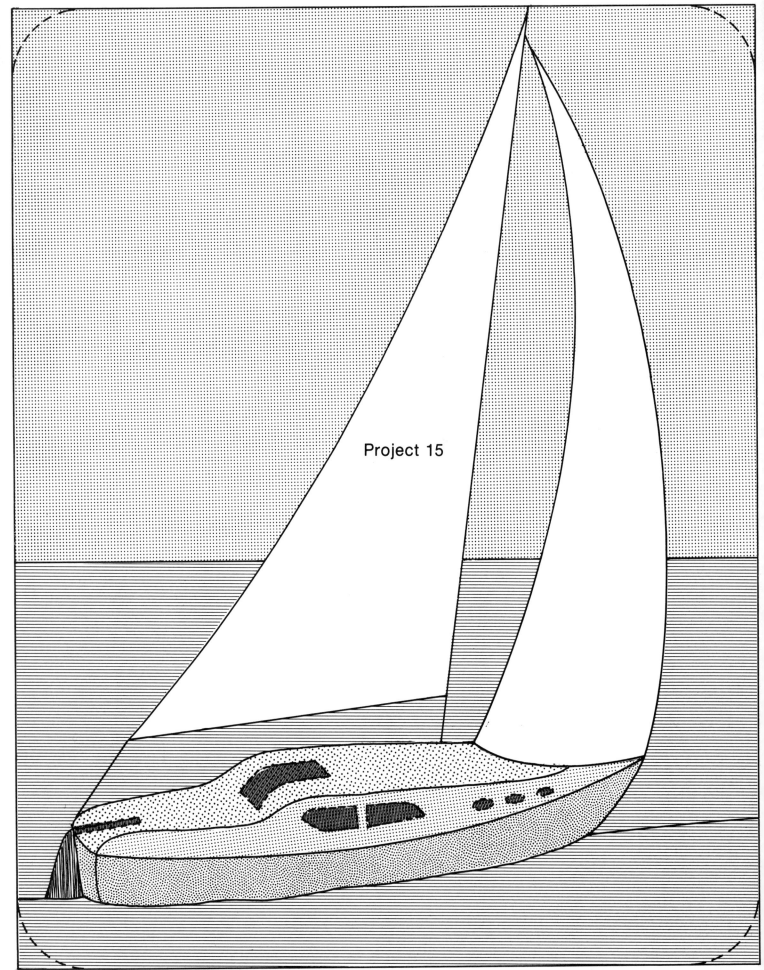

Project 15

Introduction to Stained Glass

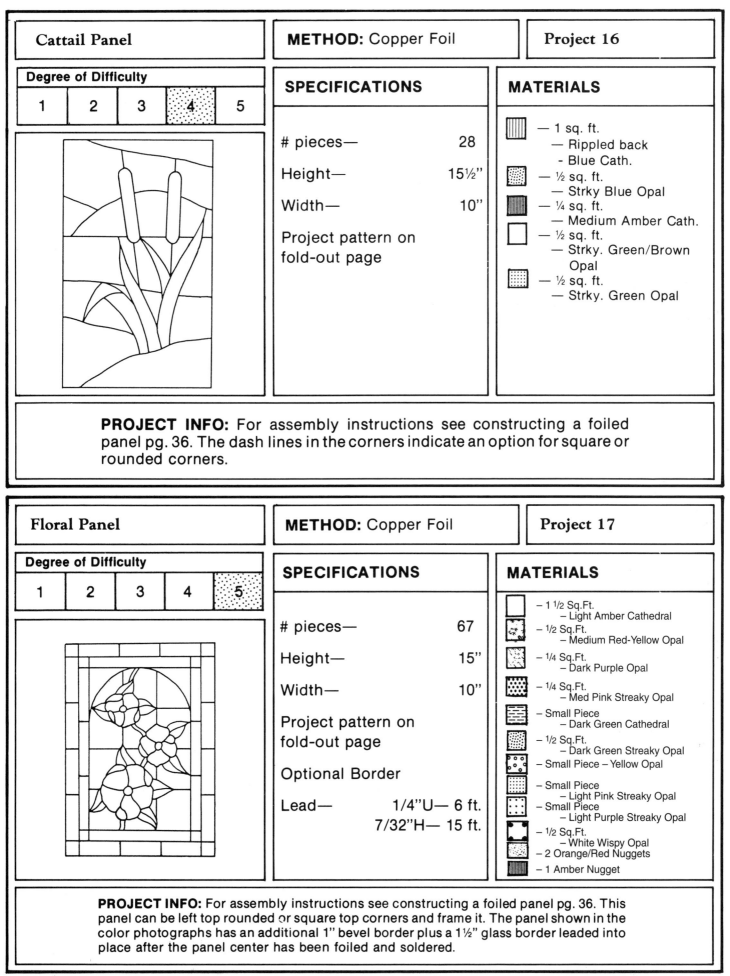

Cattail Panel	**METHOD:** Copper Foil	Project 16

Degree of Difficulty

1	2	3	4	5

SPECIFICATIONS

pieces— 28

Height— 15½"

Width— 10"

Project pattern on fold-out page

MATERIALS

— 1 sq. ft.
  — Rippled back
  - Blue Cath.
— ½ sq. ft.
  — Strky Blue Opal
— ¼ sq. ft.
  — Medium Amber Cath.
— ½ sq. ft.
  — Strky. Green/Brown Opal
— ½ sq. ft.
  — Strky. Green Opal

PROJECT INFO: For assembly instructions see constructing a foiled panel pg. 36. The dash lines in the corners indicate an option for square or rounded corners.

Floral Panel	**METHOD:** Copper Foil	Project 17

Degree of Difficulty

1	2	3	4	5

SPECIFICATIONS

pieces— 67

Height— 15"

Width— 10"

Project pattern on fold-out page

Optional Border

Lead— 1/4"U— 6 ft.
7/32"H— 15 ft.

MATERIALS

– 1 1/2 Sq.Ft.
  – Light Amber Cathedral
– ½ Sq.Ft.
  – Medium Red-Yellow Opal
– ¼ Sq.Ft.
  – Dark Purple Opal
– ¼ Sq.Ft.
  – Med Pink Streaky Opal
– Small Piece
  – Dark Green Cathedral
– ½ Sq.Ft.
  – Dark Green Streaky Opal
– Small Piece – Yellow Opal
– Small Piece
  – Light Pink Streaky Opal
– Small Piece
  – Light Purple Streaky Opal
– ½ Sq.Ft.
  – White Wispy Opal
– 2 Orange/Red Nuggets
– 1 Amber Nugget

PROJECT INFO: For assembly instructions see constructing a foiled panel pg. 36. This panel can be left top rounded or square top corners and frame it. The panel shown in the color photographs has an additional 1" bevel border plus a 1½" glass border leaded into place after the panel center has been foiled and soldered.

INDEX

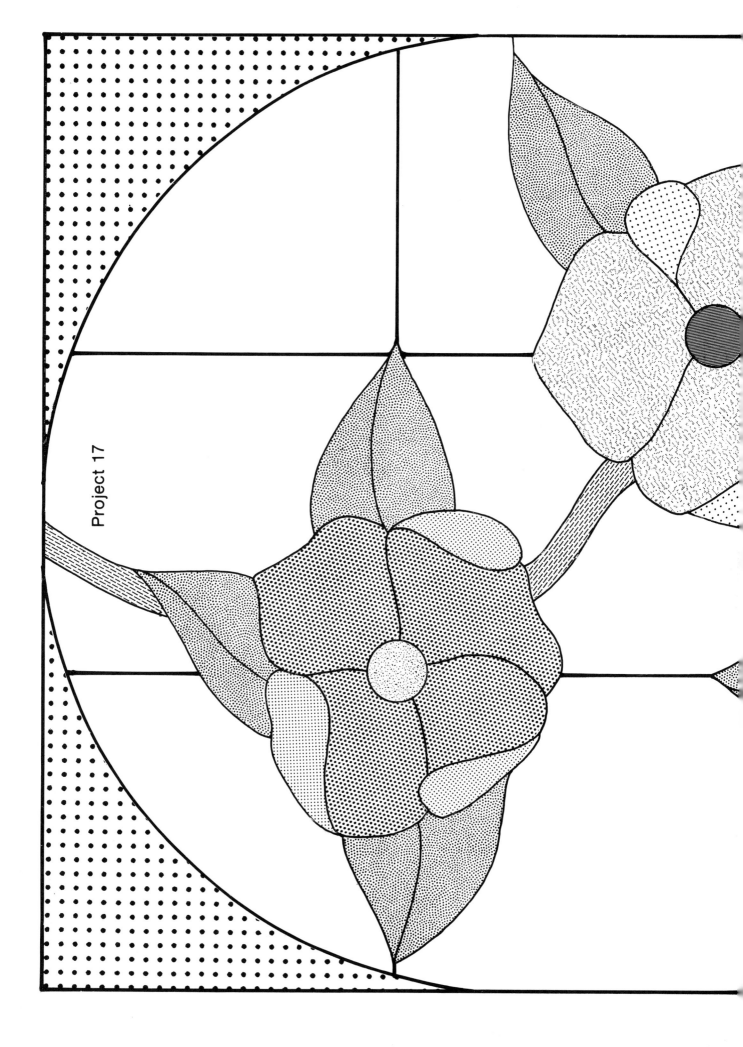

Project 17